Suddenly Unemployed

The Honest Guide to Job Searching

Richard Lowe

The Writing King

Suddenly Unemployed: The Honest Guide to Job Searching

Table of Contents

See books by Richard Lowe at

https://masterofworlds.com

5

Get free publishing insights and industry updates at

https://thewritingking.substack.com

For ghostwriting and book coaching services see

https://thewritingking.com

Disclaimer

This book provides general information and advice about job searching and unemployment. It is not intended as legal, financial, or professional career counseling advice. The author is not a licensed attorney, financial advisor, or certified career counselor.

Employment laws, unemployment benefits, disability accommodations, and workplace regulations vary significantly by state, country, and jurisdiction. Readers should consult with qualified professionals for advice specific to their legal, financial, or employment situations.

The strategies and advice in this book are based on general principles and the author's observations. Individual results may vary. No employment outcome is guaranteed by following the advice in this book.

Some company names, websites, and resources mentioned may change or become unavailable after publication. Readers should verify current information independently.

The author and publisher disclaim any liability for decisions made or actions taken based on the information in this book. Readers assume full responsibility for their career decisions and job search activities.

Introduction: Welcome to the Worst Club You Never Wanted to Join

You got fired. Or laid off. Or your contract ended. Or your company "restructured" you out of existence. The exact details don't matter. What matters is that you're unemployed, and you're feeling like your life just exploded.

Nobody prepares you for this. One day you're a professional with a title, responsibilities, and a paycheck. The next day you're unemployed, and everything you thought you knew about yourself and your future has been turned upside down.

This book isn't going to blow sunshine up your ass about how unemployment is "an opportunity for growth" or "a chance to find your passion." Unemployment sucks. It's stressful, demoralizing, and financially terrifying. Anyone who tells you otherwise has either never been unemployed or is selling you something.

What this book will do is give you a realistic roadmap for surviving unemployment and finding work again. Not inspirational platitudes. Not feel-good nonsense. Practical advice from someone who understands what you're going through.

Who This Book Is For

This book is for people who are unemployed and want to get back to work. It's for people who are tired of generic career advice that doesn't address the reality of job searching when you're desperate, broke, and running out of options.

It's for the marketing manager who got laid off after 15 years and doesn't know how to network when all their contacts work at the company that just fired them.

It's for the recent college graduate who discovered that "entry-level" jobs require three years of experience and is living in their childhood bedroom wondering if their degree was a waste of money.

It's for the 50-year-old accountant who's been told they're "overqualified" for every job they can find and is starting to wonder if their career is over.

It's for anyone who's ever stared at a job posting that perfectly describes their background and gotten rejected without explanation.

Why You Should Listen to Me

I spent 20 years as Director of Computer Operations at Trader Joe's, a $16 billion company with 38,000 employees and 474 stores. I hired people. I fired people. I sat across the table and decided in the first 30 seconds whether a resume was worth my time. I know exactly what hiring managers are thinking because I was one for two decades.

When I left Trader Joe's in 2013, I had to rebuild my professional identity from scratch — the same thing you're doing now. I've been the desperate one refreshing my inbox, the one who had to figure out how to explain a gap, the one who had to start over at an age when most people assume the hard part is behind them.

Since then I've helped hundreds of professionals reinvent themselves. I've optimized over 300 executive profiles, watched people go from overlooked to recruited, and helped clients land everything from venture capital to TEDx stages.

That's the combination this book comes from: the hiring manager who read your resume, the job seeker who started over, and the career strategist who's helped others do the same.

How to Use This Book

This book is organized roughly in the order you'll encounter challenges during unemployment. Start with the early chapters if you're newly unemployed and dealing with immediate damage control. Jump to later chapters if you've been unemployed for a while and need help with interviewing or negotiating.

Every chapter can stand alone, so don't feel like you need to read everything in order. If you're drowning in financial stress, go straight to the money chapters. If you're getting interviews but no offers, focus on the interview chapters.

The book includes advice for different situations: young people just starting their careers, older workers dealing with age discrimination, people changing industries, and those whose careers might be obsolete.

Some advice will apply to your situation, some won't. Take what's useful and ignore the rest. Your unemployment is unique to you, and your solution will be too.

If you just lost your job today and you're reading this in a panic, skip ahead to Chapter 1. It covers exactly what to do in the next 48 hours.

The Hard Truth

Unemployment isn't fair. Good people get fired for bad reasons. Qualified candidates get rejected for jobs they could do in their sleep. The process is frustrating, demoralizing, and often arbitrary.

You can't control what happened to you, and you can't control how employers respond to your applications. What you can control is your strategy, your presentation, and your mindset.

This book will help you control what you can control and navigate what you can't. It won't make unemployment easy or fun, but it will make it manageable.

Most people find work. The goal isn't to enjoy unemployment or find meaning in it. The goal is to get employed again with your finances, sanity, and relationships as intact as possible.

The Shock - What Just Happened and What You Do Right Now

You're reading this because you just lost your job. You got fired, laid off, or furloughed and now realize it's permanent. Your company went out of business or "restructured" and your position vanished. Or you quit because you couldn't take it anymore. Whatever happened, your world just got turned upside down.

You feel like you got punched in the gut. Your heart is racing, your hands are shaking, and there's a good chance you feel like you're going to throw up. This is normal. Losing your job is traumatic, whether it was your fault, their fault, or nobody's fault. Even if you chose to quit, you're second-guessing that decision.

Your brain isn't working. You can't think straight. You keep replaying what just happened in your head, or you're staring at the wall trying to process it. This is shock, and it makes people do stupid things they regret later.

Before we talk about anything else, let's talk about what you need to do in the next 48 hours to not make things worse while your brain is scrambled.

Everyone says "don't panic," but you're going to panic anyway. That's fine. Panic for a few hours, cry if you need to, punch a pillow, whatever helps. Just don't make any big decisions while you're panicking.

Don't post on social media about how your company screwed you over (or how you showed them). Don't send angry emails to your former boss. Don't call your mom crying unless she's the type who will make you feel better instead of worse. Don't make any financial decisions yet.

The urge to do something, anything, is overwhelming when you're in shock. Resist it. The best thing you can do is nothing permanent.

Let's talk about what just went down. Someone sat you down and told you that you no longer have a job. If you got fired, they used phrases like "we're going in a different direction" or "this isn't working out." If you got laid off, they talked about "budget constraints" or "organizational restructuring" or "right-sizing." If you got furloughed, they said it was "temporary" but now you know it's not. If you quit, you said something you can't take back, or you just couldn't stand another day in that place.

They were either nice about it or cold as ice. Some managers handle job cuts well, most don't. Some companies are professional about it, others are brutal. Companies going out of business or in financial trouble are often the worst about it because they're panicking too. If you quit in anger, your boss was either relieved or tried to talk you out of it.

None of that matters.

What matters is understanding exactly what they told you about your last day, your final paycheck, your benefits, and any severance package. If you were too shocked to take notes during the meeting, join the club. Most people don't retain much when they're losing their job. If you quit on the spot, you don't even know what you're entitled to.

If you got laid off, you're dealing with signing a severance agreement you don't understand. If you got furloughed, you're confused about whether you still technically work there. If the company went under, you don't know if you're getting paid at all. If you quit without notice, you're wondering if they'll even pay you for your last week.

Within the next day or two, you need to get clear on the practical stuff. If you didn't get it in writing during the termination meeting, contact HR and ask for written confirmation of your termination date, final pay date, information about continuing your health insurance, and details about any severance pay.

You have a right to this information. Don't feel like you're bothering them by asking. They ended your employment (or you did), but they still have to answer your questions about final pay and benefits.

Find out when your computer access and company email will be cut off. If it hasn't happened already, save any personal files or contacts you need. Don't take anything belonging to the company, but get your own stuff.

You need to tell a few people what happened, but choose carefully. You don't need to tell everyone.

Start with whoever handles your family's finances. If you're married, your spouse needs to know now. If you're single but your parents help with money or cosigned loans, they should know soon.

Don't call your best friend at work to vent. They're still employed there (maybe), and anything you say will get back to management. Keep your mouth shut about your former employer for now, especially if you quit in a dramatic fashion.

You're starting to do math in your head. How much money do you have? How long will it last? What about the mortgage, the car payment, the credit cards? If you quit without another job lined up, this panic is even worse.

This is when the real panic sets in. We'll deal with the money situation properly in the next chapter, but for now, know that you have more options than you think. You're not going to be homeless next week.

Don't start cutting up credit cards or selling stuff. Don't raid your savings account to pay bills that aren't due yet. Don't call the bank to explain your situation. Just breathe.

Sleep and Eat

This sounds stupid, but you need to sleep and eat. Shock and stress mess with your basic functions. You don't feel hungry, or you stress-eat everything in sight. You lie awake all night, or sleep for 14 hours.

Try to eat something with protein. Try to sleep at least six hours. Your brain needs to function well enough to make decisions over the next few weeks.

You don't have to figure out your entire life tomorrow. You don't have to start job hunting tomorrow. You don't have to update your resume tomorrow.

Tomorrow, you can start dealing with the practical stuff like unemployment benefits and health insurance. Tomorrow, you can start thinking about money. Tomorrow, you can start planning.

But tonight? You're allowed to be in shock. You're allowed to feel scared and angry and confused. You just lost your job, and that sucks no matter what the circumstances were.

Job loss feels like rejection, even when it's about budget cuts or corporate reorganization. It feels personal, even when it's not. It feels like failure, even when you did nothing wrong. If you got laid off along with 500 other people, it still feels like they picked you specifically. If you quit because the job was destroying your mental health, you still feel like you failed.

Those feelings are real and they're valid. Don't let anyone tell you to "look on the bright side" or that this is "an opportunity in disguise." It just sucks, and it's okay to feel that way.

The good news is that this feeling won't last forever. The panic will fade, your brain will start working again, and you'll figure out what comes next. But for now, just get through today.

Don't Be an Idiot - What Not to Do When You're Angry and Stupid

You're pissed off. I get it. You want everyone to know how unfair this is. You want revenge. You want to tell the world exactly what you think of your former boss and that toxic company. You want to record a TikTok in your car crying about how they screwed you over. You want to blast them on LinkedIn. You want to make them pay.

Don't.

I know you're angry. I know you feel wronged. I know you want justice. But making a public scene about your firing is career suicide, and you're too angry right now to make good decisions.

Here's what not to do while you're busy being pissed off.

Skip recording yourself getting fired. Skip the TikTok about it. Skip livestreaming your reaction. Skip posting a video of yourself crying in your car in the company parking lot. I don't care how many views and sympathy comments you think you'll get. Future employers will see it, and they'll think you're unstable and unprofessional.

Nobody wants to hire someone who might record them and put it on the internet if things go bad. Your viral moment will follow you for years. Companies Google potential employees now, and that video of you having a breakdown will be the first thing they see.

Avoid writing a manifesto about your former employer on LinkedIn. Avoid airing your grievances on Facebook. Skip tweeting a thread about what really happened. Pass on leaving Glassdoor reviews full of personal attacks. Post nothing while you're this angry.

You think you're being brave and speaking truth to power. You're burning bridges and looking petty. Other people in your industry will see it. People who might have hired you will see it.

Recruiters will see it and move on to candidates who don't come with drama.

Resist sending your coworkers long emails about what really happened. Resist texting them asking if they think it was fair. They still work there, they're scared for their own jobs, and they don't want to get involved in your drama.

The people you thought were your friends at work will distance themselves from you. That's not because they're bad people, it's because they're protecting themselves. Don't take it personally, and don't make it worse by putting them in an awkward position.

Skip calling your former boss to "tell them what you really think." Skip the angry emails to HR. Pass on writing letters to the CEO. Skip the nasty voicemails. Never show up at the office to "clear the air." You will accomplish nothing except making yourself look unstable.

Your former employer has moved on. They're not sitting around feeling guilty about firing you. They're not going to suddenly realize they made a mistake and beg you to come back. All you're doing is giving them more evidence that they made the right decision.

Avoid bad-mouthing your former employer in job interviews. When interviewers ask why you left your last job, they're not looking for the real story. They want to see if you can be professional about a difficult situation. If you launch into a story about how unfair it was, they'll assume you'll do the same thing about them someday.

Never lie about being fired. Say you were "laid off due to budget cuts" or "the position was eliminated" or "it wasn't a good fit." Keep it short, professional, and move the conversation to what you can do for them.

Hold off on major financial decisions while you're angry. Cash out your 401k to pay bills? Bad idea. Sell your car or cancel your insurance or max out credit cards in a panic? Worse idea. Cancel subscriptions you might need? Your brain isn't working clearly right now.

Resist taking the first job offer you get just to spite your former employer. Accepting a terrible job just because you want to show them you landed on your feet will backfire. Making career decisions based on anger or wounded pride lands you in an even worse situation.

Keep showing up for your own life. Keep showering and getting dressed. Stay out of bed during the day. Don't push away friends and family who are trying to help. Depression and anger feed off each other, and you need support right now.

Stop refreshing your former company's website or stalking your former coworkers on social media. Stop obsessing over whether they've posted your job yet or who they hired to replace you. Torturing yourself by staying plugged into a place that doesn't want you anymore helps nobody.

Skip hiring a lawyer unless you have a real case for wrongful termination. Most firings are legal, even when they feel unfair. Don't waste money you don't have on a lawyer who will take your case knowing you probably won't win. If you think you have a legitimate case, get a consultation, but don't sue out of spite.

Resist burning through your emergency fund on stupid stuff. Skip expensive trips to "treat yourself." Buying things to make yourself feel better is expensive therapy. Ordering takeout every night because you're too depressed to cook will drain your savings. You're going to need that money.

Keep up with your health. Keep taking medications. Don't skip doctor's appointments because you don't have insurance yet. Pain or symptoms don't disappear because you're stressed. Drinking yourself into oblivion every night won't help. You need to be functional for the job search ahead.

Be honest with your family about how bad the situation is. Pretending everything is fine when it's not just delays the inevitable conversation. Hiding the firing from your spouse or partner makes things worse. Keeping secrets about money prevents them from helping. They need to know what's happening so they can help and make adjustments.

Stop comparing yourself to people who seem to have it easier. Stop scrolling through LinkedIn seeing everyone else's career updates and promotions. Reading about people who love their jobs while you're unemployed is just self-torture. Your situation is temporary, but it won't feel that way if you keep reminding yourself of what you don't have.

Look, I know this all sounds like I'm telling you to swallow your pride and take it. I'm not. I'm telling you to be smart about your anger. Channel it into something useful: motivation to find a better job or fuel for starting your own business.

But right now, while you're raw and furious and not thinking clearly, the best thing you can do is shut up and wait. Your anger is valid, but acting on it while you're unemployed will only make things worse.

Save the revenge fantasies for after you land somewhere better. The best revenge is success, not a viral video of you crying in your car.

Money Panic - How Long Can You Actually Survive?

Let's talk about money. Not the motivational bullshit about "abundance mindset" or "money being just energy." Let's talk about cold, hard reality. How much money do you have? How long will it last? What happens when it runs out?

You're doing math in your head right now, and it's making you sick to your stomach. That's normal. Money panic is real, and it's scary as hell when you don't have income coming in.

Before you spiral into complete financial terror, let's figure out your real situation. Not the best-case scenario where you find a job next week. Not the worst-case scenario where you're homeless by Christmas. The real situation.

Grab a calculator, pull up your bank accounts, and let's do this.

Your Emergency Fund (If You Have One)

If you have money saved in a savings account, checking account, or under your mattress, that's your first line of defense. How much is it? Write that number down.

If the number is zero, don't panic yet. Most Americans have less than $1,000 in savings, so you're not alone. If you have a few thousand, that's good but not as good as you think. If you have six months of expenses saved, you're ahead of 90% of people, but you still need to be smart about it.

Don't blow through your emergency fund paying bills that aren't due yet. Don't use it to maintain your exact same lifestyle while you look for work. That money needs to last, and you don't know how long this is going to take.

Unemployment Benefits (Apply Today)

File for unemployment benefits today. Not tomorrow, not next week, today. Even if you think you won't qualify, apply anyway.

Even if you quit, apply anyway. Even if you were fired for cause, apply anyway. Let them tell you no.

The process takes weeks, and you won't get paid for the first week in most states. The sooner you apply, the sooner money starts coming in. The application is online, it takes about an hour, and it's free money the government owes you.

Unemployment pays about half your previous salary, up to a maximum amount by state. It's not enough to maintain your lifestyle, but it's enough to keep you from drowning while you figure out what's next.

If your claim gets denied, appeal it. If you're not sure how to apply, call the unemployment office. If the website crashes, try again later. Don't give up on free money because the process is annoying.

Your 401k and Retirement Accounts

Here's something most people don't know: you can access your retirement money when you lose your job. It's not ideal, but it's possible, and it might be the difference between keeping your house and losing it.

If you're 55 or older and you lost your job, you can withdraw from your 401k without the usual 10% penalty. You'll still pay income taxes, but no penalty. This is called the "Rule of 55" and it's a lifesaver for older workers who get laid off.

If you're under 55, you can still get your money, but it's more complicated. You can roll your 401k into an IRA for more options on early withdrawal. IRAs have exceptions for health insurance premiums when you're unemployed, medical expenses, and first-time home purchases.

Yes, you'll pay taxes and maybe penalties. Yes, it's not great for your retirement. But if the choice is between tapping your retirement account and losing your house, tap the retirement account. You can rebuild it later.

Don't cash out everything at once. Withdraw only what you need to survive. The rest can stay invested and keep growing.

Health Insurance (COBRA vs Everything Else)

Your health insurance ended the day you got fired, or it will end at the end of the month. You have options, but they're all expensive.

COBRA lets you keep your current insurance by paying the full premium yourself. This is expensive as hell because your employer was picking up most of the cost. But if you or your family have ongoing medical issues, it might be worth it to keep the same doctors and coverage.

You can also buy insurance through the healthcare marketplace. Losing your job counts as a "qualifying life event," so you don't have to wait for open enrollment. You might qualify for subsidies based on your new lower income.

Short-term health insurance is cheaper but covers less. It's catastrophic coverage to keep you from going bankrupt if you get hit by a bus.

If you're young and healthy, you might risk going without insurance for a few months. I don't recommend it, but I understand why people do it. If you have kids or chronic health conditions, find coverage somehow.

Credit Cards and Debt

Your credit cards can be a financial lifeline or a death trap, depending on how you use them. If you have available credit, that's an emergency fund you can tap. But credit card interest rates will destroy you if you're not careful.

Use credit cards for necessities: food, utilities, gas, minimum payments on other debts. Don't use them to maintain your lifestyle or buy things to make yourself feel better.

If you can't make minimum payments on your debts, call your creditors before you miss payments. Many will work with you on payment plans or temporary deferrals if you explain the situation. Missing payments destroys your credit score and makes everything more expensive later.

Student loans often have forbearance or deferment options for unemployed borrowers. Call your loan servicer and ask about your options. Don't just stop paying and hope for the best.

Your House and Car

If you have a mortgage, call your lender as soon as you lose your job. Many have hardship programs for temporarily reducing or deferring payments. Don't wait until you're already behind on payments.

If you rent, talk to your landlord. Some will work with you on payment plans, especially if you've been a good tenant. Others are assholes who will start the eviction process immediately. Know which one you're dealing with.

Your car payment is often one of your biggest expenses after housing. If you can't afford it, consider selling the car and buying something cheaper. Having a reliable car is important for job searching, but having a car payment you can't afford is worse.

The Math

Here's how to figure out how long your money will last:

- Add up all your available money: savings, checking, unemployment benefits, any other income.
- Add up your absolute minimum monthly expenses: rent/mortgage, utilities, food, insurance, minimum debt payments, gas. Cut everything else.
- Divide your available money by your minimum monthly expenses. That's how many months you can survive.

If the number is less than three months, you're in emergency mode. You need income fast, even if it's not your ideal job. If it's three to six months, you have some breathing room but need to be careful. If it's more than six months, you're in good shape but don't get complacent.

The Spending Rules

While you're unemployed, every dollar you spend should be questioned. Is this necessary for survival? Is this necessary for finding a job? If the answer to both is no, don't spend it.

Cut subscriptions you don't need. Cancel gym memberships. Stop eating out. Shop at discount grocery stores. Buy generic brands. Postpone anything that isn't urgent.

This isn't permanent. Once you're working again, you can go back to your normal spending. Right now, you're in survival mode.

Income You Forgot About

Check if you have money coming in: tax refunds, insurance payments, freelance work you already completed, expense reimbursements from your former employer.

If you have vacation time or sick leave your employer has to pay out, that money should show up in your final paycheck. Some states require payout, others don't.

If you worked overtime or had commissions pending, follow up on that money. Companies sometimes "forget" to pay terminated employees what they're owed.

The Bottom Line

Money panic is terrifying, but it's manageable if you're realistic about your situation. Don't pretend you have more time than you do, but don't assume you're going to be homeless next month either.

Most people find new jobs within three to six months. Plan for six months of expenses, hope for three, and prepare for longer if you're in a specialized field or difficult job market.

The goal isn't to maintain your previous lifestyle while unemployed. The goal is to survive financially until you can get back on your feet. Cut expenses, maximize income, and don't make the situation worse with panic spending or ignoring the problem.

You have more options than you think, but you need to act fast and be realistic about your situation. The money panic will fade once you have a plan and start taking action.

The Psychological Grind - When the Search Becomes a Slog

The first week of unemployment feels like a crisis. The third month feels like a prison sentence. Nobody warns you about that shift.

The initial shock eventually fades. The money panic either stabilizes or it doesn't, but either way you stop shaking every time you check your bank account. What replaces the panic is something quieter and more corrosive: the grind. Applications going nowhere. Silence from employers. A growing suspicion that something is wrong with you specifically. Days that blur together. A version of yourself you don't fully recognize.

This chapter is about that. Not the crisis, but the slog. The psychological toll of extended unemployment is real, it's common, and most career books pretend it doesn't exist.

Your Identity Just Got Mugged

Most people answer the question "who are you?" with what they do for a living. You're a project manager. An accountant. A marketing director. Take that away and the question becomes genuinely confusing.

Unemployment strips away professional identity faster than most people expect. The title, the business card, the place to be on Monday morning — all of it gone. What's left feels uncomfortably thin. You're not depressed, exactly. You just don't know how to answer basic questions about yourself anymore.

This is normal. It's also worth being honest about, because people who pretend they're fine when they're not make worse decisions. They take the wrong job out of desperation. They blow up interviews because their confidence has quietly collapsed. They isolate instead of networking, and then wonder why nothing is moving.

Acknowledging that your identity took a hit isn't weakness. It's the first step to not letting it tank your search.

The Rejection Accumulation Problem

One rejection is disappointing. Ten rejections is a pattern you start to believe. Fifty rejections — most of them silent, never even a no — starts to feel like a verdict on your worth as a person.

It isn't. The hiring process is broken in ways that have nothing to do with you. ATS systems reject qualified people automatically. Hiring managers ghost candidates after promising to follow up. Jobs get posted and then quietly filled internally. You can do everything right and still hear nothing for weeks.

The problem is that your brain doesn't know that. Your brain keeps score. It registers every unanswered application as a small personal failure, and after enough of them, the accumulated weight starts affecting your behavior. You start hedging in interviews. You apologize for gaps before anyone asks. You undersell yourself preemptively because you've been conditioned to expect the worst.

The fix isn't positive thinking. The fix is separating process from outcome. You control how many applications go out, how well your resume is tailored, how prepared you are for interviews. You do not control whether any individual employer responds. Track your inputs, not just your results. A week where you did the right things but heard nothing is still a good week.

Relationships Under Pressure

Unemployment is hard on relationships in ways nobody talks about. The financial stress is obvious. The identity stuff is less obvious but just as damaging.

Partners and spouses often don't know how to help, so they ask questions that feel like pressure: any leads today? did you apply anywhere? what's the plan? They mean well. It feels like interrogation. You start avoiding conversations about the job search, which means you start avoiding conversations generally, which means the relationship quietly deteriorates.

Friends who are employed start to feel like a different species. Their problems are about performance reviews and office politics. Yours are about whether you can make rent. The gap is real and it creates distance even when everyone is trying.

The temptation is to isolate. Don't. Isolation makes everything worse and it kills your network at the exact moment you need it most. Instead, be direct with the people close to you about what kind of support actually helps. Some people need their partner to stop asking daily updates and just trust the process. Some people need a friend who will take them to lunch and not mention the job search for an hour. Know what you need and ask for it specifically.

Structure Is Not Optional

Work provides structure you don't notice until it's gone. A reason to get up. A place to be. A sequence of tasks. A social context. When all of that disappears, days stop having edges. Monday feels like Thursday. Morning bleeds into afternoon. A week goes by and you're not sure where it went or what you actually did.

Unstructured time feels like freedom at first. After a few weeks it feels like quicksand.

Treat the job search like a job. Set a start time and an end time. Give yourself a daily task list and actually complete it. Take a real lunch break. Get dressed — not necessarily in business clothes, but in something that signals to your brain that the day has started. These aren't productivity hacks. They're mental health maintenance.

Build in things that have nothing to do with finding a job. Exercise. A project. Volunteering. Something that produces a visible result and gives you a reason to leave the house. The job search can consume everything if you let it, and that level of obsession makes you worse at it, not better.

When It Becomes Something More

Stress and sadness during unemployment are normal. Clinical depression is something different, and the line between them can blur over weeks of rejection and isolation.

Signs that what you're experiencing has moved beyond situational stress: you can't get out of bed most days, not just occasionally. You've stopped doing things you normally enjoy, completely, for weeks. You can't concentrate well enough to complete a job application. You're drinking more, or using anything else to get through the day. You're having thoughts about harming yourself.

If any of those describe you, the job search needs to take a back seat temporarily. You cannot interview well, network effectively, or make good decisions about your career when your mental health is in crisis. Getting help is not a detour from finding work. It's a prerequisite.

Community mental health centers offer sliding-scale or free therapy. Open Path Collective connects people with therapists who charge reduced rates. The 988 Suicide and Crisis Lifeline is available by call or text if things get acute. Your former employer's Employee Assistance Program may still cover a limited number of therapy sessions after termination — check your severance paperwork.

The Thing Nobody Says Out Loud

Most people who go through extended unemployment come out the other side changed in ways they didn't expect. Some of those changes are bad — lasting anxiety about job security, a lower baseline confidence that takes years to rebuild. Some are genuinely useful — a clearer sense of what actually matters, less tolerance for jobs or workplaces that are bad for you, a practical toughness that only comes from having survived something hard.

You don't have to reframe this as a gift. It's not a gift. But it's also not permanent. The grind ends. Most people find work. The identity reassembles itself around new facts. The relationships that survived the stress are often stronger for it.

Right now your job is to keep moving without letting the psychological weight stop you. That's harder than it sounds and more important than most of the tactical advice in this book.

Fast Money - Side Gigs That Actually Pay This Week

You need money coming in fast. Not next month, not when you find the perfect job, but this week. While you're applying for unemployment and figuring out your long-term plan, you need cash flow to keep the lights on.

Here's the deal: there are ways to make money quickly if you're willing to work and not too proud to do whatever it takes. Most of them won't replace your previous salary, and some of them suck. But sucking is better than starving.

Here's what can put money in your pocket within days, not weeks.

Gig Economy Work

The gig economy exists for situations like yours. Companies need workers, you need money, and you can start making cash almost immediately.

Drive for Uber or Lyft if you have a decent car and clean driving record. You can start earning money within a few days of signing up. The pay varies wildly depending on your location and when you drive, but you can make $15-25 an hour during busy times. Drive during rush hours, weekend nights, and special events for the best money.

Deliver food with DoorDash, Uber Eats, or Grubhub if your car isn't nice enough for passengers. Food delivery is less picky about your vehicle and you don't have to talk to drunk people. The money is similar to rideshare, but you'll put more miles on your car.

Shop for other people with Instacart or Shipt. Grocery shopping pays decent money, especially if you're good at finding items quickly and can handle heavy lifting. Some shoppers make $20-30 an hour during busy periods.

Walk dogs or pet-sit through Rover or Wag. If you like animals and live in an area with busy pet owners, this can pay well. Dog walking pays $15-30 per walk, and overnight pet-sitting can bring $50-100 per night.

Treat gig work like a real job. Work during peak hours, learn your market, and track your expenses for taxes. Don't just drive around randomly hoping for rides.

Freelance Your Skills

If you have any marketable skills, freelancing can pay much better than driving for Uber. It takes longer to build up clients, but you might land something quickly.

Writing and editing work is everywhere if you can string sentences together. Content mills like Textbroker and WriterAccess pay quickly but not much. Better-paying gigs are on Upwork, Freelancer, or by directly contacting businesses that need help with their websites or marketing.

Graphic design, web development, and digital marketing skills are in high demand. Even basic WordPress or social media management can pay $25-50 an hour. Post your services on Fiverr, Upwork, or local Facebook groups.

Tutoring or teaching can bring good money if you're knowledgeable in any subject. Online tutoring through Wyzant or Tutor.com lets you work from home. Local tutoring pays better but takes longer to set up.

Handyman work, cleaning, or other physical services can start paying immediately. Post on Craigslist, TaskRabbit, or Thumbtack. People always need help moving, cleaning, or fixing things.

Sell Your Knowledge

If you have expertise in anything, people will pay for advice or training.

Consulting in your field can pay your old hourly rate or higher. Reach out to your network and let them know you're available for project work. Even if companies aren't hiring full-time, they might need help with projects.

Create and sell online courses about what you know. Platforms like Teachable or Udemy let you upload courses quickly. It takes time to build an audience, but once it's set up, it's passive income.

Offer workshops or training sessions for local businesses or organizations. Many companies need help with software, processes, or skills training.

Quick Cash Jobs

Some work pays cash the same day you do it.

Day labor through temp agencies can put money in your pocket daily. Construction, warehouse work, and event staffing often pay at the end of each shift. It's not glamorous, but it's immediate money.

Plasma donation pays $20-50 per session, and you can donate twice a week in most places. It's not a job, but it's regular money for something your body makes anyway.

Participate in paid research studies or focus groups. Universities, market research companies, and medical facilities pay participants for studies. Some pay $50-200 for a few hours of your time.

Seasonal work picks up quickly. Tax season, holiday retail, summer landscaping, or event staff for weddings and parties. These jobs often hire fast and pay weekly.

Online Opportunities

The internet offers ways to make money from home, though many are small amounts that add up.

Take online surveys through Swagbucks, Survey Junkie, or Prolific. You won't get rich, but you can make $50-100 a month clicking buttons while watching TV.

Sell photos you've taken through stock photo sites like Shutterstock or Adobe Stock. If you have a decent camera or smartphone and an eye for composition, people buy photos for websites and marketing.

Virtual assistant work is growing as more businesses operate remotely. Help with email management, scheduling, data entry, or customer service. Sites like Belay and Time Etc hire virtual assistants.

Transcription work through Rev or TranscribeMe pays for typing up audio recordings. It's tedious but you can work whenever you want.

Turn Hobbies Into Cash

Look at what you already know how to do and figure out how to monetize it.

If you're crafty, sell handmade items on Etsy, Facebook Marketplace, or local craft fairs. Jewelry, art, home decor, and custom items can bring good money.

Photography services for events, portraits, or real estate. Everyone needs photos, and many photographers charge $100-300 for basic sessions.

Cooking or baking for others. Meal prep services, custom cakes, catering for small events. Check local regulations about selling food from home.

Music lessons, either in person or online. If you play any instrument, people will pay to learn.

The Reality Check

Most of these options won't replace a professional salary, but they can cover basic expenses while you job hunt. Start multiple income streams and be realistic about what you can earn.

Don't quit job searching to focus on gig work unless the gig work is paying better than you expect to make in your next job. These are bridges, not destinations.

Track everything for taxes. Gig work income is taxable, and you'll need records. Set aside 20-30% of what you make for taxes since nobody is withholding them for you.

Watch your expenses. Gas, car maintenance, and equipment costs can kill your earnings if you're not paying attention.

Getting Started Fast

Pick two or three options that match your skills and situation. Apply for everything at once since some take longer to approve than others.

Set up profiles on multiple platforms. Don't put all your eggs in one basket. Uber might not have enough rides in your area, but food delivery might be busy.

Start immediately. The longer you wait, the longer it takes to see money. Even if you only make $20 your first day, that's $20 you didn't have.

Be professional even in gig work. Show up on time, communicate clearly, and do good work. Good ratings lead to more opportunities and better pay.

The goal is getting money flowing while you work on finding a real job. Fast money isn't usually good money, but it beats no money while you figure out what's next.

Your Reputation and What People Will Think

Everyone's going to know you got fired. The question is what story they hear and who they hear it from first. You can either sit back and let other people control the narrative, or you can get out ahead of it and manage your reputation like a professional.

You have about 48 hours before word spreads through your industry. Use them.

Make the Calls (Today)

Before you do anything else, before you update your LinkedIn, before you start applying for jobs, you need to make phone calls. Pick up the phone and call six people who matter in your professional life. Not emails, not texts, phone calls.

Call your most important industry contacts, former colleagues who've moved to other companies, clients you had good relationships with, mentors, anyone who might hear about your situation and whose opinion affects your career.

The conversation is simple: "Hi, I wanted to let you know that I'm no longer with [Company]. The position was eliminated due to budget cuts." (Or whatever your professional version of the story is.) "I'm going to be exploring new opportunities and I wanted you to hear it from me first."

That's it. Don't over-explain. Don't vent. Don't ask for anything. Just give them the facts before someone else gives them gossip.

Some of these calls will turn into longer conversations about opportunities. Some people will offer to help. Some will just say "thanks for letting me know" and that's fine too. The point is that they heard your version first.

Make these calls on the day you get fired or the next day at the latest. Every day you wait is another day for rumors to spread without your input.

LinkedIn Overhaul

Your LinkedIn profile is about to get a lot more attention. People will be checking to see if you've updated it, what you're saying, how you're handling the transition. Make it work for you.

Update your headline immediately. Don't leave it as your old job title because that looks like you haven't figured out what's happening. Don't write "Seeking new opportunities" because that screams desperation. Write something that positions you for what you want next: "Marketing Leader | Brand Strategy & Digital Growth" or "Operations Executive | Process Optimization & Team Leadership."

Rewrite your summary to focus on your value and what you're looking for. "Experienced project manager with a track record of delivering complex initiatives on time and under budget. Interested in opportunities to lead cross-functional teams in fast-growing companies." Keep it forward-looking, not backward-looking.

Update your location and contact information. Make sure people can reach you. Add your personal email and phone number since your work contact information is gone.

Change your profile photo if it's outdated or unprofessional. You want to look current and polished, not like someone who hasn't updated anything in three years.

Post an update about your availability, but make it strategic. Don't post "I got laid off, please help me find a job." Post something like "After three successful years at [Company], I'm excited to explore new opportunities in [industry/function]. I'm interested in roles where I can leverage my experience in [key skills]. Open to conversations about interesting challenges."

Strategic Social Media Cleanup

Go through your Facebook, Twitter, Instagram, and any other social media accounts. You're about to have potential employers looking at everything.

Facebook: Tighten your privacy settings so only friends can see your posts. Clean up your profile picture and cover photo to look professional. Remove or hide any posts that make you look unprofessional. You don't have to be boring, but drunk party photos aren't helping your job search.

Twitter: If you tweet about work-related topics, make sure your bio reflects your current situation and what you're looking for. If you don't tweet professionally, consider making your account private.

Instagram: Clean up anything that's obviously unprofessional. Most employers won't dig deep into Instagram, but if your account is public and easy to find, make sure it doesn't hurt you.

Google yourself and see what comes up. If there's negative information about your departure you can't control, start creating positive content to push it down in the search results.

Networking Without Looking Desperate

Being unemployed makes networking feel awkward because you obviously need something. The key is networking strategically without looking like you're just trolling for job leads.

Join or become more active in professional associations. Attend industry events, even virtual ones. Participate in online discussions in your field. The goal is staying visible and engaged, not hiding until you find a new job.

Reach out to people in your network regularly, but don't always ask for something. Share interesting articles, make introductions between people who should know each other, congratulate people on promotions or new roles. Be useful to your network, not just a drain on it.

When you do reach out for help, ask for advice, not jobs. "I'm exploring opportunities in fintech and I know you've worked in that space. Do you have 15 minutes to share your thoughts on the industry?" People are more willing to give advice than job leads, and advice conversations often turn into job leads anyway.

Follow up with people, but don't be annoying about it. If someone doesn't respond to your first message, wait at least two weeks before trying again. If they don't respond to the second message, move on.

Reference Strategy

Figure out who's going to vouch for you and make sure they're prepared to do it well.

Identify 4-5 people who can speak positively about your work. This should include former managers, colleagues, clients, and maybe someone from a different department who can speak to your collaboration skills.

Reach out to each potential reference personally. Explain that you're job searching and ask if they'd be comfortable serving as a reference. Give them context about the types of roles you're pursuing so they can tailor their comments.

Send each reference your updated resume and a brief summary of your accomplishments they witnessed. Most people want to help but they might not remember specific details about projects you worked on together.

Don't use your most recent boss as a reference if you think they'll say anything negative. It's better to explain why you're not using them than to let them sabotage your chances.

Managing the Rumor Mill

In small industries, everyone knows everyone. You can't control what people say about you, but you can influence it.

Be visible and professional in your interactions. The best counter to negative rumors is consistently demonstrating that you're reasonable, competent, and easy to work with.

Don't respond to every piece of gossip or try to correct every misunderstanding. It makes you look defensive and keeps negative stories alive longer than necessary.

If someone asks you directly about what happened, give them the same professional explanation you've prepared. Don't get into the details of workplace drama or personality conflicts.

Content Strategy While Unemployed

Stay active on LinkedIn with thoughtful content related to your industry. Share interesting articles with your commentary, write posts about industry trends, engage meaningfully with other people's content.

The goal is staying top of mind with your network and demonstrating your expertise, not announcing your job search every day.

Don't post about being unemployed more than once. One professional post about exploring new opportunities is enough. After that, focus on sharing value and engaging with others.

Comment thoughtfully on other people's posts. It's a low-key way to stay visible without constantly posting your own content.

Playing the Long Game

Your reputation isn't just about managing the immediate aftermath of losing your job. It's about positioning yourself as someone people want to work with and hire.

Help other people when you can. Make introductions, share job postings that aren't right for you, offer advice to people who reach out. Being generous with your network while you're unemployed shows character and keeps you top of mind for opportunities.

Volunteer for industry organizations or causes related to your field. It keeps your skills sharp, gives you something positive to discuss in interviews, and shows that you're proactive and engaged.

Attend industry events and conferences, even if you have to pay for them yourself. Staying connected to your professional community is an investment in your career, not an expense.

Consider speaking at events or writing articles about your area of expertise. Thought leadership activities position you as an expert and keep you visible in your field.

The Follow-Up System

Keep track of everyone you talk to and follow up systematically. Use a spreadsheet or CRM to track conversations, follow-up dates, and what each person might be able to help with.

Send thank-you notes after networking conversations. It's basic politeness and it keeps you in people's minds.

Update your network on your job search progress occasionally, but don't spam them with constant updates. A brief note every month or two letting people know you're still looking and what types of opportunities interest you is plenty.

When you do land a new job, make sure to thank everyone who helped along the way. Your network will remember how you handled your job search, and it affects how willing they'll be to help you in the future.

Your reputation is one of your most valuable career assets. Manage it actively, not passively. The effort you put into relationship management while you're unemployed will pay dividends for years to come.

Why Your Resume Probably Sucks and How to Fix It

Your resume sucks. I don't need to see it to know this. Most people's resumes are terrible, outdated, boring documents that sound like they were written by a robot having a nervous breakdown.

The resume you used to get your last job won't get you your next job. The rules changed completely in the last few years, and most people are still writing resumes like it's 2015. If you're unemployed and using an old resume, you're showing up to a gunfight with a slingshot.

Here's why your resume sucks and how to fix it before you send it to anyone who matters.

The Problems with Most Resumes

Your resume is boring. It reads like every other resume the hiring manager has seen this week. "Detail-oriented professional with excellent communication skills seeking a challenging opportunity to leverage my experience in a dynamic environment." Nobody cares. This tells me nothing about what you've done or what you can do for them.

Your resume is the wrong length. If you've been working for more than five years and your resume is one page, you're leaving out important stuff. If your resume is more than two pages and you're not a doctor or professor, you're including too much irrelevant stuff.

Your resume focuses on responsibilities instead of accomplishments. "Responsible for managing a team of five people" tells me nothing. Did the team succeed? Did they fail? Did you fire everyone and start over? "Led a team of five that increased sales by 30% in six months" tells me what you can do.

Your resume has no keywords. Applicant tracking systems (ATS) scan resumes for specific words before humans ever see them. If your resume doesn't include the right keywords from the job posting, it gets rejected automatically. You'll never know why you didn't hear back.

Your resume is generic. You're using the same resume for every job application. Marketing jobs need different keywords and emphasis than operations jobs. One-size-fits-all resumes fit nobody well.

Your contact information is wrong or incomplete. You still have your work email from the job you just lost. Your LinkedIn URL is the generic one with random numbers. Your phone number goes to voicemail with an unprofessional message.

What Works Now

Modern resumes need to pass ATS systems first, humans second. This means your beautiful formatting, fancy fonts, and creative layouts are hurting you. ATS systems can't read them properly and will reject your resume before anyone sees it.

Use a simple, clean format. Black text on white background. Standard fonts: Arial, Calibri, or Times New Roman. No graphics, no text boxes, no fancy headers. Save the creativity for your portfolio or cover letter.

Include a professional summary at the top, but make it specific to what you're applying for. Instead of generic fluff, write 2-3 sentences about your experience and what you want to do next. "Operations manager with 8 years of experience streamlining manufacturing processes and reducing costs. Led teams that decreased production time by 25% while maintaining quality standards. Seeking senior operations role in growing manufacturing company."

Focus on accomplishments with numbers. Don't just list what you did, show what you achieved. "Managed social media accounts" becomes "Increased social media engagement by 150% and grew followers from 5,000 to 25,000 in 12 months." "Handled customer service" becomes "Maintained 95%

customer satisfaction rating while resolving 50+ customer issues daily."

Every bullet point should start with an action verb and include a measurable result when possible. Managed, led, created, developed, implemented, increased, decreased, improved, launched, designed. Skip the passive language and weak verbs like "helped with" or "assisted in."

Use keywords from the job posting. If the job description mentions "project management" five times, make sure those words appear in your resume. If they want experience with specific software, list that software if you've used it. Don't lie, but don't make them guess whether you have the skills they want.

The Modern Resume Structure

Contact information at the top: name, phone, email, city and state, LinkedIn URL. Skip the full address unless the job requires local candidates. Use your personal email, not your work email. Make sure your LinkedIn URL is customized, not the random string of numbers LinkedIn assigns.

Professional summary: 2-3 sentences about your experience and what you're looking for. This should be customized for each job application.

Core competencies or skills section: 8-12 keywords and skills relevant to the job you're applying for. This helps with ATS scanning and gives the hiring manager a quick overview of what you can do.

Professional experience: List your jobs in reverse chronological order. For each job, include company name, your title, dates, and 3-5 bullet points about your accomplishments. Focus on the last 10 years unless older experience is directly relevant.

Education: Degree, school, graduation year. If you graduated more than 10 years ago, you can skip the year. If you have relevant certifications or professional development, include them here.

Skip the references line. Everyone knows you'll provide references if asked. Use that space for something more useful.

Writing Better Bullet Points

Bad: "Responsible for managing the marketing budget" Good: "Managed $500K annual marketing budget, reducing costs by 15% while increasing lead generation by 40%"

Bad: "Worked with cross-functional teams" Good: "Collaborated with engineering, design, and product teams to launch three new features, resulting in 25% increase in user engagement"

Bad: "Handled customer complaints" Good: "Resolved customer escalations within 24 hours, improving customer retention rate from 85% to 92%"

Bad: "Organized company events" Good: "Planned and executed quarterly company events for 200+ employees, staying within budget while achieving 95% attendance rate"

The formula is: Action verb + what you did + measurable result. If you can't measure the result, explain the impact or scope of what you did.

Tailoring for Each Job

Read the job posting carefully. Highlight the keywords, skills, and requirements they mention. Make sure your resume includes as many of those keywords as honestly possible.

Reorder your bullet points to put the most relevant experience first. If they want project management experience, lead with your project management accomplishments even if that wasn't your main responsibility.

Adjust your professional summary for each application. If you're applying for a marketing role, emphasize your marketing experience. If you're applying for an operations role, focus on your operations background.

Don't lie, but do emphasize the experience that's most relevant to what they're looking for. If you managed a team for six months out of a three-year role, but they want management experience, make sure that six months is prominently featured.

Common Mistakes That Kill Your Chances

Using an objective statement instead of a professional summary. "Seeking a challenging position where I can grow my skills" tells them nothing about what you can do for them. Focus on what you offer, not what you want.

Including irrelevant personal information. Your marital status, religion, political affiliation, and hobbies have no place on your resume unless they're directly relevant to the job. Save the space for professional accomplishments.

Using passive language. "Was responsible for" and "duties included" make you sound like you just showed up and didn't accomplish anything. Use active verbs that show you took initiative and got results.

Including too much old experience. If you're applying for a director-level position, nobody cares that you were a great cashier in college 15 years ago. Focus on experience that's relevant to where you want to go, not where you've been.

Spelling errors and typos. This is an automatic disqualifier for most employers. Use spell check, read it out loud, and have someone else review it before you send it anywhere.

Getting Past the ATS

Most companies use applicant tracking systems to filter resumes before humans see them. Here's how to get past the robots:

Use standard section headings. "Professional Experience" instead of "Where I've Worked." "Education" instead of "Learning Journey." ATS systems look for specific headings and might not recognize creative ones.

Include both acronyms and spelled-out versions of important terms. "Project Management Professional (PMP)" instead of just "PMP." "Customer Relationship Management (CRM)" instead of just "CRM."

Use standard file formats. PDF is usually safe, but Word documents are more reliably readable by ATS systems. Check the job posting to see if they specify a format.

Don't get creative with formatting. Tables, text boxes, headers, and footers can confuse ATS systems. Stick to simple formatting that any system can read.

The Cover Letter Question

Most cover letters are worthless. "I am writing to express my interest in the position" is not a compelling opening. If you're going to write a cover letter, make it count.

Use it to tell a story your resume can't tell. Explain why you're changing industries, why you're interested in their company, or how your background gives you a unique perspective on their challenges.

Keep it short. Three paragraphs maximum. One to grab their attention, one to explain why you're a good fit, one to close and request an interview.

Don't just repeat what's on your resume. The cover letter should add context and personality your resume doesn't provide.

Many applications don't even ask for cover letters anymore. If it's optional, skip it unless you have something genuinely compelling to say.

Testing Your Resume

Before you send your resume anywhere, test it. Copy and paste the text into a plain text document. If it's unreadable, the ATS can't read it either.

Run it through an ATS checker online. There are free tools that will scan your resume and tell you how well it matches a job posting.

Have someone else read it. Fresh eyes catch things you miss. Ask them to explain what you do for work based on your resume. If they can't, rewrite it.

Apply for a few jobs you don't really want to test how your resume performs. If you're not getting any responses, the problem is your resume, not the job market.

Your resume is your marketing document. It needs to sell your accomplishments and get you interviews. If it's not doing that, fix it before you waste time applying to jobs with a broken tool.

How to Take Advantage of AI for Your Job Search

AI is everywhere now, and everyone's telling you to use it for your job search. Most of the advice is terrible. "Just ask ChatGPT to write your resume!" "Let AI craft the perfect cover letter!" "Use machine learning to find your dream job!"

This is like saying "just use the internet" to solve all your problems. AI tools can be useful for job searching, but only if you know what they're good at and what they're not.

Here's how to use AI effectively in your job search without looking like an idiot or getting caught using obviously generated content.

What AI Does Well

AI excels at certain tasks that are tedious, time-consuming, or require processing lots of information quickly. It's terrible at things requiring judgment, creativity, or understanding human nuance.

AI is good at analyzing job descriptions, suggesting keywords, organizing information, generating first drafts, researching companies, and identifying patterns across large datasets.

AI is bad at understanding company culture, reading between the lines in job postings, knowing what hiring managers want, creating authentic personal stories, and making strategic career decisions.

Understanding this difference determines whether AI helps your job search or hurts it.

Resume Optimization (The Right Way)

Don't ask AI to write your resume from scratch. It will produce generic garbage that sounds like every other AI-generated resume.

Use AI to analyze job descriptions and identify important keywords you might have missed. Feed it the job posting and your current resume, then ask what keywords and skills from the posting aren't reflected in your resume.

Use AI to suggest different ways to phrase your accomplishments. If you wrote "managed a team," AI can suggest alternatives like "led," "supervised," "directed," or "coordinated." This helps you avoid repetitive language.

AI can help you tailor your resume for different roles. Show it two different job descriptions and ask how you should emphasize different aspects of your experience for each role.

Always review and edit everything. AI doesn't understand which of your experiences are most impressive or relevant. It can't judge whether a suggested change makes you sound more or less qualified.

Cover Letters That Don't Suck

The worst thing you can do is ask AI to write your entire cover letter. Hiring managers are getting dozens of obviously AI-generated letters that all sound the same.

Use AI to research the company and role. Ask it to summarize recent news about the company, explain their business model, or identify their main challenges. This gives you talking points for your cover letter.

Ask AI to help you structure your letter. Give it your key selling points and ask for an outline that flows logically. Then write the content yourself.

Use AI to improve your draft after you've written it. Ask it to make your language more concise, suggest stronger action verbs, or identify places where you're being too generic.

The goal is using AI to enhance your authentic voice, not replace it with robotic corporate speak.

Job Search Strategy and Organization

AI can help you stay organized and strategic about your job search in ways that matter.

Use it to track your applications. Set up a system where AI helps you log where you've applied, what stage each application is in, and when to follow up.

Ask AI to analyze patterns in job postings. Feed it 20 job descriptions for roles you want and ask what skills, qualifications, and keywords appear most frequently. This shows you what to emphasize.

Use AI to research salary ranges. While sites like Glassdoor exist, AI can analyze multiple sources and give you a broader picture of compensation for roles in your location.

Get help prioritizing applications. Give AI your criteria (salary range, company size, location) and ask it to help you rank opportunities based on how well they match your requirements.

Interview Preparation

AI can be useful for interview prep, but not in the way most people think.

Don't just ask AI for generic interview questions. Research the company and role, then ask AI to generate questions that company would likely ask based on their business model and challenges.

Use AI to practice explaining complex technical concepts in simple terms. If your job involves specialized knowledge, practice explaining it to AI and ask for feedback on clarity.

Ask AI to help you develop examples for behavioral interview questions. Give it your work history and ask for suggestions on which experiences best demonstrate leadership, problem-solving, or teamwork.

Use AI to research your interviewers. If you know who you're meeting with, ask AI to help you find appropriate information about their background and interests.

Networking and Outreach

AI can help you network more effectively, but subtlety is key.

Use AI to help craft LinkedIn connection requests. Give it context about how you know the person and why you want to connect, then ask for a brief, personalized message.

Ask AI to help you identify mutual connections. Feed it someone's LinkedIn profile and yours, then ask for suggestions on how to get an introduction.

Use AI to research networking events and professional associations in your field. Ask for recommendations based on your location and industry.

Get help crafting follow-up messages after networking events. Give AI context about your conversation and ask for suggestions on how to continue the relationship.

Company Research

This is where AI really shines. It can process vast amounts of information about companies much faster than you can.

Ask AI to summarize a company's recent financial performance, major initiatives, and competitive challenges. This gives you intelligent talking points for interviews.

Use AI to identify companies you might not have considered. Describe your ideal work environment and ask for suggestions of companies that match those criteria.

Research company culture through AI analysis of employee reviews, social media presence, and public communications. AI can identify patterns and themes you might miss.

Ask AI to help you understand how your skills translate to different industries. Feed it your background and ask which industries might value your experience.

The Things You Shouldn't Do

Don't submit AI-generated content without heavily editing it. Hiring managers are getting better at spotting artificial writing, and it makes you look lazy or dishonest.

Don't rely on AI for strategic career decisions. AI can give you information and options, but it can't decide what's best for your situation and goals.

Don't use AI to fake knowledge or experience you don't have. It might help you write about skills convincingly, but you'll be exposed quickly in interviews or on the job.

Don't trust AI's advice about salary negotiations or offer evaluation without verification from other sources. AI doesn't understand local market conditions or company factors.

Staying Human in an AI World

The biggest risk of using AI in your job search is losing your authentic voice and personal connection with potential employers.

Hiring is fundamentally about human relationships. Companies hire people they like and trust, not just qualified candidates. AI can help you get noticed, but it can't build relationships for you.

Use AI as a research assistant and writing coach, not as a replacement for your own thinking and judgment. The best applications of AI enhance your natural abilities instead of replacing them.

Be prepared to talk about your AI usage honestly if asked. Many companies are curious about how candidates use AI tools, and being thoughtful about it can be a positive.

The Practical Workflow

Here's a realistic way to incorporate AI into your job search:

Start each application by using AI to analyze the job description and suggest relevant keywords for your resume. Spend 10 minutes on this, not an hour.

Use AI to research the company and generate 3-4 talking points for your cover letter. Then write the letter yourself using your authentic voice and experiences.

Before interviews, ask AI to generate potential questions based on the company and role. Practice your answers out loud, not just in writing.

After networking events, use AI to help you craft personalized follow-up messages. Always add something from your conversation.

Use AI to track and organize your job search activities. Let it handle the administrative stuff so you can focus on relationship-building and strategic thinking.

The Future Reality

AI is becoming part of the hiring process on both sides. Companies are using AI to screen resumes, analyze video interviews, and assess candidates. Understanding this helps you navigate it better.

Optimize your resume for AI screening systems by including relevant keywords and using standard formatting. Don't sacrifice readability for humans.

In video interviews that use AI analysis, maintain good eye contact with the camera, speak clearly, and use confident body language. AI systems often analyze these factors.

Be prepared for AI-assisted interview questions. Some companies use AI to generate personalized questions based on your resume and their needs.

The Bottom Line

AI is a tool, not a magic solution for job searching. It can make you more efficient and organized, help you identify opportunities you might miss, and improve your written communications.

It can't replace the human elements that matter most: building relationships, demonstrating authentic expertise, and showing genuine enthusiasm for opportunities.

Use AI to handle the mechanical parts of job searching so you can spend more time on the human parts. That's where you'll find the real advantage.

The candidates who succeed will be those who use AI thoughtfully to enhance their job search while maintaining their authenticity and personal connections. Don't let technology replace the fundamentals of good job searching. Let it make them more effective.

The Job Search That Actually Works

Forget everything you know about job searching. The advice your parents gave you is outdated. The strategies that worked five years ago are mostly useless now. If you're sitting at your computer scrolling through job boards and clicking "apply" on dozens of postings, you're wasting your time.

Online job applications have become the equivalent of buying lottery tickets. Sure, someone wins occasionally, but your odds are terrible and you're competing with thousands of other people for the same positions. Most of the jobs you see posted online are already filled or will be filled through internal referrals and networking.

Here's what modern job searching looks like and how to do it right.

Why Job Boards Don't Work

Job boards are where careers go to die. Indeed, LinkedIn Jobs, ZipRecruiter, all of them. They're designed to make money for the platforms, not to help you find work.

Companies post jobs because they have to. HR departments need to show they conducted a "fair and open" search. Legal departments want documentation that they considered external candidates. But most hiring managers already know who they want to hire before the job gets posted.

The math is brutal. A typical job posting gets 250+ applications. Maybe 10 people get phone screens. Maybe 3 get interviews. Maybe 1 gets the job. You're competing with hundreds of people, most of whom are equally qualified.

Applicant tracking systems filter out most resumes before humans see them. If your resume doesn't have the exact keywords they're looking for, or if the ATS can't parse your formatting, you're rejected automatically. You won't even know why.

Even if you get past the ATS, your resume lands in a pile with 50 others. The hiring manager spends 30 seconds scanning each one. Unless something jumps out immediately, you're in the "no" pile.

The jobs posted online are usually the ones they couldn't fill through networking. Think about what that means. The good jobs, the ones with reasonable managers and decent company cultures, get filled before they're ever posted publicly.

The Hidden Job Market

Most jobs are never advertised. Studies show that 70-80% of positions are filled through networking, internal referrals, or direct recruiting. These are the jobs you want.

Hidden jobs happen when someone leaves unexpectedly, when a department gets more budget, when a project needs staffing, when someone gets promoted and creates an opening. The manager thinks "who do I know who could do this?" or asks their team "do you know anyone good?"

Companies prefer to hire people who come recommended because it reduces risk. If Jane from accounting vouches for you, you're not going to be a disaster. Referrals also save time and money on recruiting.

Internal candidates get first shot at openings. If they can promote from within or transfer someone from another department, they will. External hiring is expensive and uncertain.

Direct recruiting happens when companies need specific skills. They use LinkedIn to find people who aren't job searching but might be interested in the right opportunity. These "passive candidates" are often the most desirable because they're currently employed and successful.

The Real Job Search Strategy

Your job search should be 20% applications and 80% networking and relationship building. This is The Job Search Inversion — and it runs counter to everything your instincts tell you to do.

When you lose your job, every instinct says to act — send more applications, apply to more postings, do more of what feels like work. That impulse produces the wrong result. The jobs that get filled publicly are the ones companies couldn't fill privately. You're competing for leftovers. The Job Search Inversion means deliberately spending most of your time on the activity that feels less productive — conversations — and less time on the activity that feels most productive — applications. This is not intuitive. Do it anyway.

Start with your existing network. Make a list of everyone you know professionally: former colleagues, clients, vendors, people from industry events, classmates, neighbors who work in your field. Don't pre-filter this list. Include people you haven't talked to in years.

Reach out to 5-10 people per week. Not to ask for jobs, but to reconnect and let them know you're looking for opportunities. The conversation should be: "Hi, I'm exploring new opportunities after leaving [Company]. I'd love to catch up and hear what you're working on these days."

Most people will ask what kind of opportunities you're looking for. Have a clear, specific answer ready. Not "anything in marketing" but "senior marketing manager roles at B2B tech companies, focused on demand generation and growth marketing."

Ask for advice, not jobs. "I'm targeting fintech companies and I know you've worked in that space. What should I know about the industry right now?" People are more comfortable giving advice than making referrals to strangers.

Follow up consistently. If someone gives you advice or makes an introduction, send a thank-you note and update them on your progress. Most job seekers disappear after the first conversation, which wastes the relationship.

LinkedIn as a Job Search Tool

LinkedIn is not a job board. It's a networking platform that happens to have job postings. Use it for relationship building, not just applications.

Optimize your profile for search. Recruiters use LinkedIn to find candidates, so make sure they can find you. Use keywords from job descriptions in your headline and summary. Include skills and technologies you want to work with.

Post regular updates about your job search and industry insights. "Exploring opportunities in data analytics. Interested in companies using AI to solve real business problems." This keeps you visible to your network and shows you're actively looking.

Engage with other people's content. Comment thoughtfully on posts from people in your industry. Share interesting articles with your perspective. This keeps you on people's radar without being pushy about your job search.

Use LinkedIn's advanced search to find people at companies you're interested in. Look for alumni from your school, former colleagues who moved to those companies, or people with similar backgrounds. Send personalized connection requests.

Join LinkedIn groups in your industry. Participate in discussions, share valuable content, and connect with other members. Many groups have job sharing threads where members post opportunities at their companies.

Direct Outreach

Research companies you want to work for and reach out directly, even if they don't have posted openings. Many companies are always open to good people, especially if you bring skills they need.

Find the hiring manager for the type of role you want. This is usually someone with a director or VP title in the relevant department. LinkedIn makes this easy if you know the company name and function.

Send a brief, personalized message. Mention something specific about the company that interests you. Explain what you do and ask if they have any current or upcoming needs in your area.

Don't attach your resume to the first message. It makes the outreach feel like spam. If they're interested, they'll ask for it. Keep the initial message conversational and focused on learning about their needs.

Follow up if you don't hear back. People are busy and messages get buried. A polite follow-up after a week shows persistence without being annoying.

Target growing companies and startups. They're more likely to have unposted openings and less rigid hiring processes. A 50-person company might create a new role if they find the right person.

Working with Recruiters

Third-party recruiters can be valuable allies, but you need to work with them strategically. Not all recruiters are worth your time.

Find recruiters who specialize in your industry and function. A recruiter who focuses on marketing roles at tech companies understands your market better than someone who recruits for everything.

Build relationships with 3-5 good recruiters. Keep them updated on your search and be responsive when they reach out about opportunities. Good recruiters will think of you when the right role comes up.

Be clear about what you want. Give them specific parameters: company size, industry, role level, compensation range, location preferences. Vague requests get vague results.

Don't rely entirely on recruiters. They're working for the companies that pay them, not for you. Use them as one channel among many, not your primary strategy.

Be wary of recruiters who want to "represent" you exclusively or who ask you to sign contracts. Good recruiters earn their fees by making successful placements, not by locking you into agreements.

The Application Strategy

When you do apply for posted jobs, be strategic about it. Don't spray and pray. Target roles where you're a strong fit and can make a compelling case.

Read the job description carefully. If you don't meet at least 70% of the requirements, don't bother applying. You're wasting everyone's time, including your own.

Customize your resume for each application. Use keywords from the job posting. Reorder your bullet points to emphasize relevant experience. Write a targeted professional summary.

If you have a connection at the company, mention it in your cover letter. "Jane Kowalski suggested I apply for this role" gets attention. Even better, ask Jane to forward your resume directly to the hiring manager.

Apply early. Most hiring managers review applications as they come in. Being in the first batch is better than being in the pile of 200 applications that arrived later.

Follow up strategically. If you haven't heard anything after a week, try to find the hiring manager on LinkedIn and send a brief note expressing continued interest.

Informational Interviews

Informational interviews are underused and highly effective. The goal is to learn about companies and roles while building relationships with people who might hire you or refer you later.

Target people whose jobs you want or who work at companies you're interested in. Ask for 15-20 minutes to learn about their career path and get advice about the industry.

Prepare thoughtful questions. Ask about their role, what they like about the company, what challenges they're facing, what skills are most important for success. Show genuine interest in their insights.

Don't ask for a job during an informational interview. It violates the implied agreement and makes people uncomfortable. Focus on learning and relationship building.

Follow up with a thank-you note and stay in touch periodically. Share interesting articles or updates on your job search. These relationships often lead to referrals months later.

Many informational interviews turn into job opportunities. If the person likes you and a role opens up, you'll be top of mind.

Industry Events and Networking

Attend industry conferences, meetups, and professional events. Virtual events count too. The goal is meeting people and staying visible in your professional community.

Prepare your elevator pitch. You need a 30-second explanation of who you are, what you do, and what you're looking for. This is a version of the 30-Second Bridge from the interviews chapter — the same structure works in networking conversations: what you were doing, what you're looking for next, and why that specific person or company is interesting to you. Practice it until it sounds natural, not rehearsed.

Follow up with everyone you meet. Connect on LinkedIn within 24 hours with a personalized note referencing your conversation. Most people don't do this, so you'll stand out.

Volunteer for industry organizations. It's a great way to meet people while demonstrating your skills and commitment to the field.

Speaking at events positions you as an expert and creates opportunities for people to approach you. Start small with local meetups or panel discussions.

The Long Game

Job searching is a numbers game, but it's not about the number of applications you submit. It's about the number of meaningful professional relationships you build and maintain.

Track your networking activities. Keep a spreadsheet of who you've talked to, when you last connected, and any follow-up actions needed. Relationship management is part of the job search process.

Be helpful to others. Share job postings that aren't right for you, make introductions between people who should know each other, offer advice to other job seekers. What goes around comes around.

Stay visible in your industry even when you're not job searching. The best time to build your network is when you don't need it. The relationships you build now will help with your next job search.

Most people find their next job through relationships, not applications. Invest your time accordingly. The job search that works is the one focused on people, not postings. And if after 60 days nothing is moving, use the Three-Lever Diagnosis in the conclusion to identify exactly which part of your approach is broken — targeting, materials, or relationships — instead of trying to fix everything at once.

Job Searching with ADHD

If you have ADHD, job searching feels like it was designed by someone who hates you personally. Everything about the process works against how your brain operates. Applications require sustained attention to boring details. Interviews demand sitting still and making small talk. Networking events are sensory nightmares.

The career advice industry pretends ADHD doesn't exist or treats it like a minor inconvenience you can overcome with better planning. That's garbage. ADHD affects how you process information, manage time, handle rejection, and maintain motivation. Ignoring these realities sets you up for failure.

This chapter addresses the specific challenges ADHD creates during job searching and provides strategies that work with your brain instead of against it.

Why Traditional Job Search Advice Fails ADHD Brains

Most job search advice assumes you can sit down, make a plan, and execute it systematically over weeks or months. It assumes you can handle boring, repetitive tasks without losing focus. It assumes rejection won't send you into a shame spiral that derails your entire search.

These assumptions are wrong if you have ADHD.

Your brain craves novelty and stimulation. Filling out identical application forms feels like torture. Your working memory struggles with multi-step processes, so you forget to follow up on applications or miss interview preparation steps. Time blindness makes deadlines feel either impossibly far away or suddenly urgent with no middle ground.

Executive function challenges affect every part of job searching. You might hyperfocus on perfecting a resume for hours while ignoring dozens of job opportunities. Or you might apply to jobs impulsively without researching the companies, then feel overwhelmed by the response.

Rejection sensitivity makes each "no" feel personal and devastating. What neurotypical job seekers experience as mild disappointment can trigger intense shame and self-doubt that stops your search for days or weeks.

The ADHD Advantage in Job Searching

ADHD isn't just a collection of challenges. Your brain also has superpowers that can give you advantages in the right situations.

You think creatively and make connections others miss. While other candidates give standard answers, you might approach problems from unexpected angles that impress interviewers. Your ability to hyperfocus means you can dive deep into companies and roles that interest you, preparing for interviews with enthusiasm that's hard to fake.

You adapt quickly to new situations. Many ADHD people thrive in dynamic environments and handle change better than their neurotypical colleagues. You might be naturally drawn to startups, fast-paced industries, or roles that others find too chaotic.

Your pattern recognition skills help you read people and situations quickly. You might notice things about company culture or interviewer behavior that others miss. Your intuition about whether a job or workplace will be a good fit is often accurate.

Managing the Application Process

Traditional application tracking systems and lengthy forms are ADHD kryptonite. You need systems that work with your brain's preferences for variety and immediate feedback.

Break applications into micro-tasks. Instead of "apply to 10 jobs today," try "find 3 interesting job postings" and "complete 1 application." Smaller goals feel achievable and give you frequent dopamine hits from completion.

Use the Pomodoro Technique for application marathons. Work for 25 minutes, then take a 5-minute break. This prevents the mental fatigue that leads to careless mistakes or abandoning applications halfway through.

Create templates for common application questions, but customize them for each job. Having starting points reduces the blank-page paralysis while ensuring you don't send generic responses.

Apply immediately when you find interesting jobs. Your ADHD brain is great at initial enthusiasm but terrible at sustained motivation. If you save jobs "for later," later often never comes.

Interview Strategies for ADHD

Interviews challenge multiple ADHD weaknesses simultaneously: sitting still, sustained attention, reading social cues, and managing anxiety. Preparation becomes crucial because you can't rely on thinking clearly under pressure.

Prepare stories, not just answers. ADHD brains remember narratives better than facts. Create 5-7 specific examples that demonstrate your skills and practice telling them as engaging stories. Stories also help with time blindness because narratives have natural beginnings, middles, and ends.

Practice out loud, preferably with another person. Your brain processes information differently when speaking than when thinking. What sounds clear in your head might come out jumbled when you're nervous.

Request accommodation for fidgeting if you need it. "I think better when I can move around a bit" is usually acceptable. Bring a stress ball or small fidget toy if sitting perfectly still is impossible.

Use the interviewer's energy to guide your responses. ADHD people often excel at reading nonverbal cues. If the interviewer looks engaged, continue with details. If they seem ready to move on, wrap up quickly.

Arrive early but don't go inside until 5-10 minutes before your appointment. Sitting in a waiting room for 30 minutes will drain your mental energy before the interview starts.

Networking with ADHD

Traditional networking advice tells you to work a room systematically and make small talk with strangers. For many ADHD people, this is social hell.

Focus on quality connections over quantity. Your hyperfocus ability means you can have really engaging conversations with people who interest you. Two meaningful connections are better than twenty business card exchanges.

Use your pattern recognition to identify the right people to approach. You're good at reading room dynamics and spotting the people who seem genuinely helpful versus those just collecting contacts.

Prepare conversation starters about industry trends or recent news. Having specific topics prevents the awkward "so what do you do" small talk that feels scripted and boring.

Follow up immediately after meeting someone interesting. Don't trust yourself to remember to reach out "next week." Send a LinkedIn connection or email within 24 hours while the conversation is fresh.

Choose networking events carefully. Industry meetups focused on specific topics work better than generic business mixers. Your brain engages more when there's substance to discuss.

Time Management and Organization

ADHD time management requires external structure because your internal clock is unreliable. You need systems that account for hyperfocus, procrastination, and the tendency to underestimate how long tasks take.

Use calendar blocking for job search activities. Treat job searching like a part-time job with specific hours. This prevents the all-or-nothing thinking that leads to either obsessive searching or complete avoidance.

Set up external accountability. Share your job search goals with a friend or family member who will check in regularly. Your brain responds better to external deadlines than internal motivation.

Create visual progress tracking. Use a simple spreadsheet or app to track applications, interviews, and follow-ups. Seeing progress helps maintain motivation during long job searches.

Batch similar tasks together. Do all your resume customizing in one session, all your research in another. Task-switching drains ADHD energy faster than sustained focus on one type of activity.

Handling Rejection and Setbacks

Rejection hits ADHD brains differently because of rejection sensitive dysphoria. What feels like normal disappointment to others can trigger intense shame, anger, or despair that derails your entire search.

Expect rejection to feel worse than it should. Knowing this is an ADHD thing, not a personal failure, helps you prepare coping strategies before you need them.

Create a rejection recovery routine. Have specific activities planned for after getting bad news: call a supportive friend, go for a walk, watch favorite videos, or engage in a hobby. Don't leave yourself alone with negative thoughts.

Reframe rejection as data collection. Each "no" tells you something about fit, timing, or market conditions. This intellectual approach helps counter the emotional overwhelm.

Don't job search when you're already emotionally depleted. ADHD emotional regulation is worse when you're tired, stressed, or dealing with other life challenges. Taking breaks isn't giving up; it's strategic.

Energy Management

ADHD brains have limited executive function energy that depletes throughout the day. Job searching requires significant mental resources, so you need to manage your cognitive load carefully.

Do your most important job search tasks during your peak energy hours. For most people, this is morning, but know your own patterns. Don't waste high-energy time on mindless tasks like updating your LinkedIn headline.

Minimize decision fatigue by creating routines. Wear the same type of outfit to interviews. Use the same coffee shop for application sessions. Automate what you can so your brain energy goes toward important decisions.

Take real breaks between intensive tasks. Scrolling social media isn't rest for your brain. Take walks, listen to music, or do something completely different from job searching.

Know your hyperfocus triggers and use them strategically. If researching companies sends you down rabbit holes, schedule these sessions when you have time for deep dives.

Plan for post-interview crashes. Many ADHD people feel emotionally and physically drained after interviews. Don't schedule anything important immediately afterward.

Workplace Fit Considerations

ADHD people often struggle in environments that seem perfect on paper but clash with how their brains work. Consider these factors when evaluating opportunities.

Open office environments can be sensory nightmares for ADHD people. Ask about workspace setup during interviews. Look for companies that offer quiet spaces, flexible seating, or remote work options.

Highly structured environments with rigid processes might feel suffocating. Conversely, chaotic environments with no systems might overwhelm your executive function. Look for the sweet spot of structure with flexibility.

Consider your need for variety and stimulation. Jobs with repetitive tasks might bore you quickly, while roles with too much novelty might scatter your attention. Think about what balance works for your brain.

Ask about company culture around neurodiversity. Some employers genuinely support different thinking styles; others just say they do. Look for specific examples of accommodations or flexibility they've provided.

Remote Work Considerations

Remote work can be either fantastic or terrible for ADHD people, depending on your specific challenges and home environment.

Remote work eliminates commute stress and office distractions that drain ADHD energy. You can create an environment optimized for your brain's needs. You can also work during your peak energy hours instead of fitting into traditional schedules.

But remote work also removes external structure that many ADHD people need. Without colleagues around, you might struggle with motivation or time management. The isolation can worsen rejection sensitivity or depression.

Your home environment matters enormously. If your living space is chaotic or full of distractions, remote work might not be viable. You need dedicated space and systems to separate work from personal life.

Consider hybrid arrangements that give you flexibility without complete isolation. Many ADHD people thrive with 2-3 days remote and 2-3 days in office.

Disclosure Decisions

Deciding whether and when to disclose ADHD is complex. Legal protections exist, but discrimination still happens. Consider your specific situation carefully.

You're not required to disclose ADHD during the hiring process unless it affects your ability to do essential job functions. Most ADHD people can perform job requirements with or without accommodations.

If you need accommodations, it's usually better to wait until after receiving a job offer to start disclosure conversations. This protects you from pre-employment discrimination while ensuring you get necessary support.

Common workplace accommodations include flexible schedules, quiet workspace, written instructions, modified break schedules, and noise-canceling headphones. Most accommodations cost employers nothing or very little.

Some people choose to disclose ADHD strategically as an explanation for their working style preferences. "I do my best work in the morning" or "I prefer written instructions" can be ways to get what you need without formal disclosure.

Research the company's track record on disability inclusion before making disclosure decisions. Some employers genuinely support neurodiversity; others just have policies on paper.

Building Support Systems

Job searching with ADHD is harder when you're doing it alone. Build systems and relationships that provide the external structure and emotional support your brain needs.

Find an accountability partner who understands ADHD challenges. This might be another job seeker, a friend, or a family member. Regular check-ins help maintain momentum and provide reality checks when you're catastrophizing.

Consider working with a career coach who has experience with neurodivergent clients. They can help you develop systems that work with your brain instead of against it.

Join ADHD support groups or online communities. Talking with people who understand your challenges reduces isolation and provides practical strategies.

Use your existing support network strategically. Let people know how they can help: proofreading applications, practicing interview questions, or just being available when you need to vent about rejections.

Don't try to hide your struggles from people who care about you. ADHD people often mask their difficulties, but job searching is stressful enough without pretending everything is fine.

Long-term Career Planning

ADHD affects not just job searching but career development over time. Think about how to build a sustainable career path that leverages your strengths and accommodates your challenges.

Look for growth opportunities that match your hyperfocus interests. ADHD people often excel when they're passionate about their work. Passion provides the motivation to push through boring tasks and administrative requirements.

Build skills that are transferable across roles and industries. ADHD people sometimes need to change jobs more frequently than neurotypical workers, either by choice or circumstance. Broad skills provide more options.

Consider entrepreneurship or consulting if traditional employment feels limiting. Many ADHD people thrive with more control over their work environment and schedule. But be realistic about the business skills and self-discipline required.

Develop relationships with managers who understand and support neurodiversity. Good managers can make enormous differences in your success and job satisfaction. Cultivate these relationships when you find them.

Plan for the financial reality that ADHD might affect your career trajectory. You might change jobs more often or need more time between positions. Building emergency funds and developing multiple income streams provides security.

Making It Work

Job searching with ADHD requires different strategies than conventional career advice suggests. You need approaches that work with your brain's strengths and accommodate its challenges.

The key is accepting your neurological reality instead of trying to force yourself into neurotypical systems. Your brain processes information differently, handles stress differently, and finds motivation differently. Fighting these differences wastes energy you need for the actual job search.

Focus on finding environments where your ADHD traits are assets instead of liabilities. The right workplace can make you feel like a superstar instead of a constant failure. Those workplaces exist, but you have to be strategic about finding them.

Don't let well-meaning advice from neurotypical people derail your customized approach. They mean well, but they don't understand how ADHD affects every aspect of job searching. Trust your own experience about what works for your brain.

Remember that ADHD is an explanation for your challenges, not an excuse. You still need to do the work of job searching, but you can do it in ways that set you up for success instead of struggle.

The job market needs what ADHD brains offer: creativity, adaptability, passion, and different perspectives. Your challenge is finding the people and organizations smart enough to recognize that value.

Networking When You're Desperate (and People Can Smell It)

Networking when you're unemployed feels gross. You know you need something, everyone else knows you need something, and every conversation has this underlying tension of "please help me find a job" hanging in the air. You feel like a beggar at a cocktail party.

The worst part is that people can smell desperation from across the room. You try to act casual, but your body language screams "I NEED WORK" and every conversation feels forced and transactional. You're not networking anymore, you're just hitting people up for favors.

This is exactly when networking matters most, and exactly when you're worst at it. Here's how to network effectively when you're unemployed without looking like a sad, hungry vulture circling the professional community.

Why Desperate Networking Fails

When you're unemployed, you approach networking backward. You start with what you need instead of what you can offer. Every conversation becomes about your job search, your situation, your problems. Nobody wants to be someone's career life preserver.

You rush the relationship. Instead of building genuine connections, you're speed-dating for job leads. You meet someone at a networking event and launch into your elevator pitch about being "between opportunities." They can feel you sizing them up for usefulness.

You follow up too aggressively. You connect on LinkedIn and send a message asking if their company is hiring. You send weekly "just checking in" emails that are thinly veiled job inquiries. You're not nurturing relationships, you're pestering people.

You disappear when you don't get immediate value. If someone can't help you with your job search, you lose interest in the relationship. This makes you look selfish and short-sighted, and word spreads in professional communities.

You broadcast your desperation through body language and conversation. You dominate discussions with talk about how hard the job market is, how unfair your termination was, how long you've been searching. People start avoiding you because you're an energy drain.

The Right Mindset

Networking isn't about extracting value from people. It's about building mutually beneficial relationships. When you're unemployed, you need to think longer-term even though you need short-term results.

Focus on being useful, not being helped. Ask yourself: what can I offer to other people right now? Maybe you have industry insights, maybe you know about job openings that aren't right for you, maybe you can make introductions between people who should know each other.

Think about networking as intelligence gathering, not job hunting. You're learning about industries, companies, trends, and opportunities. You're building a database of knowledge that will help you make better career decisions.

Approach conversations with genuine curiosity about other people's work. Most people love talking about what they do if you ask thoughtful questions. This makes you memorable in a good way and builds real connections.

Remember that networking relationships pay off over months and years, not days and weeks. The person you meet today might not be able to help you now, but they might think of you when something opens up in six months.

Strategic Networking When Unemployed

Be selective about events and activities. Don't just show up anywhere there might be professional people. Target events where you can provide value or learn something useful, not just collect business cards.

Prepare differently. Instead of perfecting your elevator pitch about being available for opportunities, prepare interesting questions about industry trends, company challenges, or professional development. Make conversations about them, not you.

Lead with curiosity, not availability. "I'm exploring opportunities in fintech and would love to understand the challenges facing the industry" is better than "I'm looking for a job in fintech."

Share insights and information. If you've been researching companies or industries during your job search, you have valuable intelligence. Share what you've learned about market trends, competitive dynamics, or hiring patterns.

Make introductions. Use your job search as an opportunity to connect people who should know each other. "You should meet Sarah Kimmel from TechCorp, she's working on similar challenges" creates goodwill and keeps you visible.

Online Networking Strategy

LinkedIn becomes even more important when you're unemployed, but use it strategically. Don't just post "I'm available for opportunities" every week. Share thoughtful content about your industry, comment meaningfully on other people's posts, and engage in discussions.

Join LinkedIn groups related to your field and participate in discussions. Answer questions, share resources, and provide advice to other members. This positions you as knowledgeable and helpful, not just job hunting.

Use LinkedIn to research people before events or meetings. Know who you want to meet and why. Have specific questions or topics prepared based on their background and current role.

Follow up on LinkedIn after meeting people, but don't ask for anything. Connect with a personalized note referencing your conversation, then engage with their content occasionally to stay visible.

Share other people's job postings that aren't right for you. This shows you're plugged into the market and generous with your network. People remember this kind of helpfulness.

Handling the Unemployment Question

People will ask about your employment status. Have a prepared, confident answer that doesn't make the conversation awkward or invite pity.

“I'm exploring new opportunities after leaving TechCorp” is better than “I got laid off and I'm looking for work.” The first sounds intentional, the second sounds desperate.

Keep it brief and redirect the conversation. “I'm between roles right now and taking the opportunity to meet people in the industry and learn about new trends. What's been the biggest change you've seen in your field lately?”

Don't overshare about your job search struggles or complain about the market. Nobody wants to hear about how hard it is to find work or how many applications you've submitted without responses.

If someone offers to help, be specific about what would be useful. “I'd love an introduction to anyone working in product management at mid-size SaaS companies” is more helpful than “let me know if you hear of anything.”

Working Your Existing Network

Start with people who already know and like you. Former colleagues, classmates, neighbors, friends of friends. These warm connections are more likely to help and less likely to judge your unemployment status.

Reach out with a specific agenda beyond "I'm job hunting." Ask for advice about industries or companies, request introductions to specific people, or offer to help with projects they're working on.

Give updates on your search progress, but focus on what you're learning instead of how hard it is. "I've been talking to people in the cybersecurity field and it's interesting how much the landscape has changed" is better than "I've been looking for three months and haven't found anything yet."

Be patient with people who don't respond immediately. Everyone is busy, and your job search isn't their priority. Follow up once after a reasonable time, then move on if you don't hear back.

Thank people for their help and update them on outcomes. If someone makes an introduction that leads to an interview, let them know. If you get a job through their network, send a proper thank-you note.

Industry Events and Conferences

Attend events with a learning agenda, not just a networking agenda. Pick sessions that teach you something valuable about your field. This gives you conversation starters and demonstrates your commitment to professional development.

Volunteer at events if possible. It's a great way to meet organizers and speakers, and it shows initiative. Volunteers often get better access to networking opportunities.

Prepare thoughtful questions for speakers and panelists. Ask about industry trends, not job opportunities. Good questions make you memorable and position you as engaged and knowledgeable.

Follow up with interesting people you meet, but focus on continuing the conversation instead of asking for favors. Reference something specific from your discussion to jog their memory.

Don't pitch yourself to everyone you meet. Have real conversations about their work, their company, their challenges. If there's a natural fit for further discussion, it will emerge organically.

Building Relationships, Not Extracting Favors

Think of networking as making professional friends, not collecting job leads. Professional friends genuinely care about each other's success and stay in touch.

Remember personal details about people you meet. Their kids, their hobbies, their career goals. Follow up on things they mentioned they were working on or worried about.

Celebrate other people's successes. Congratulate them on promotions, new jobs, or professional achievements. Share their good news with your network when appropriate.

Offer specific help when you can. If you see a job posting that might interest someone in your network, send it to them. If you meet someone who could help a contact, make the introduction.

Stay in touch even when you don't need anything. Send interesting articles, check in on projects they mentioned, congratulate them on company news. This keeps relationships warm for when you do need support.

Managing Rejection and Indifference

Not everyone will be helpful, and that's normal. Some people are too busy, some don't like networking, and some just aren't generous with their professional connections. Don't take it personally.

If someone doesn't respond to your outreach, don't keep pushing. Move on to other contacts and other opportunities. Persistence can quickly become harassment.

When people can't help directly, ask if they know someone who might be able to provide guidance. Most people are more comfortable making introductions than making hiring decisions.

Don't burn bridges with people who can't help you now. Your situations might change, and someone who couldn't help you today might be in a position to help you later.

Keep your network broad. Don't rely on a few key contacts to solve your job search. The more relationships you have, the more opportunities you'll hear about.

The Long-Term Perspective

Good networking relationships outlast any single job search. The people you meet while unemployed might become lifelong professional contacts who help you throughout your career.

Stay in touch with your network after you find a job. Don't be someone who disappears until they need help again. Maintain relationships when you don't need anything.

Pay it forward. When you're employed again, help other people who are job searching. Remember how it felt to need support and be generous with people who are in that position.

Build relationships in multiple industries and functions. Diversifying your network gives you more opportunities and makes you less vulnerable to downturns in any single area.

Track your networking activities and relationships. Keep notes on who you've met, how you met them, and what you talked about. This helps you follow up appropriately and maintain relationships.

Networking when you're desperate is hard, but it's also when you most need the support of your professional community. Do it right, and you'll not only find your next job faster, you'll build relationships that benefit your entire career.

Interviews When You're Coming from Unemployment

You finally got an interview. After weeks or months of applications and networking, someone wants to talk to you. You should be excited, but instead you're terrified because you know "the question" is coming.

"So, tell me about your current situation."

"I see there's a gap in your resume."

"Why did you leave your last position?"

They want to know why you're unemployed. And you have to answer without sounding desperate, bitter, or like damaged goods. You have to convince them you're worth hiring despite the fact that you don't currently have a job.

Here's how to handle interviews when you're unemployed without sabotaging your chances.

The Unemployment Stigma

Being unemployed hurts your candidacy. Employers prefer to hire people who are currently employed because it suggests someone else values your work. It's the professional equivalent of wanting to date someone who's already in a relationship.

Some hiring managers assume unemployed people are desperate and will take any offer. Others worry there's something wrong with you that caused your unemployment. The longer you've been out of work, the more these biases work against you.

You can't eliminate these biases, but you can minimize their impact by controlling the narrative and demonstrating your value despite your current status.

Preparing Your Story

Before any interview, you need a clear, confident explanation for why you're unemployed. Call this the 30-Second Bridge — a three-part structure that moves the conversation from your past to your future before the interviewer has time to linger on the gap.

Part one: what happened. Ten seconds, factual, no blame. You were laid off, the position was eliminated, the company restructured. Full stop. Don't explain, justify, or editorialize.

Part two: what you did with the time. Ten seconds. You've been selective, you've been learning, you've been consulting — something that signals forward motion rather than stagnation. Even if the honest answer is "I've been applying and getting rejected," you can frame it as being deliberate about finding the right fit.

Part three: why this opportunity specifically. Ten seconds. Something concrete about this role or this company that connects to your background. This is the pivot — you've crossed the bridge and you're no longer talking about unemployment. You're talking about the future.

The whole answer should take 30 seconds, not three minutes. Interviewers don't need the full story. They need enough to stop worrying about the gap. Here's what it sounds like:

If you were laid off: "The company eliminated my position as part of a restructuring. I'm excited about this opportunity because it lets me focus on the areas where I've had the most success."

If you were fired for performance: "The role evolved in a direction that didn't match my strengths. I learned a lot about what I want in my next position, which is why I'm interested in this opportunity."

If you quit without another job: "I decided to take some time to evaluate my career direction and explore opportunities that align better with my goals. This role is exactly what I was looking for."

Practice your story until it sounds natural and confident, not rehearsed or defensive.

The Gap Question

Interviewers will ask about employment gaps. The longer the gap, the more explaining you'll need to do.

For gaps under three months: "I'm taking my time to find the right opportunity instead of jumping into something that isn't a good fit."

For longer gaps: "I've been selective about my next move because I want to find a role where I can make a real impact. I've used this time to [skill development/networking/industry research] and I'm excited about what you're building here."

If you've been doing freelance or consulting work during your gap, mention it. Any work is better than no work in the interviewer's mind.

Don't apologize for being unemployed or act like it's a personal failing. Treat it as a normal part of career transitions.

Demonstrating Value Despite Unemployment

You need to prove you're still sharp and engaged despite not having a current job. Here's how:

Stay current with industry trends. Read industry publications, follow thought leaders, attend virtual events. Reference recent developments in your field during the interview.

Show what you've been doing with your time. Learning new skills, taking courses, working on projects, volunteering. Unemployment doesn't mean you've been sitting on the couch.

Bring energy and enthusiasm. Unemployed people sometimes seem defeated or low-energy. Show genuine excitement about the opportunity and the company.

Ask informed questions about the role and company. This shows you've done your research and are seriously interested, not just looking for any job.

Share specific examples of your accomplishments. Don't let being unemployed overshadow your track record of success.

Handling Salary Discussions

Being unemployed weakens your negotiating position, but don't give away your worth.

If they ask about salary expectations early: "I'm sure you pay competitively for this level of role. Can you tell me more about the responsibilities so I can give you a more informed answer?"

If pressed for a number: Give a range based on market rates for the role, not your desperation level. "Based on my research, similar roles in this market range from \$X to \$Y."

Don't volunteer that you'll take less because you're unemployed. Let them make the first offer, then negotiate from there.

If you're asked about your last salary: In many states, this question is illegal. If it's legal where you are, you can say "I'd prefer to focus on the value I can bring to this role instead of my previous compensation."

Common Interview Mistakes When Unemployed

Oversharing about your situation. Keep your explanation brief and professional. They don't need to know about your financial stress or family pressure.

Seeming too eager. Yes, you need the job, but desperation is unattractive. Show interest without begging.

Accepting lowball offers immediately. Being unemployed doesn't mean you have to take the first offer. You can still negotiate respectfully.

Badmouthing your former employer. Even if they treated you terribly, criticism reflects poorly on you. Take the high road.

Focusing on what the job will do for you instead of what you'll do for them. Talk about how you'll contribute, not how much you need the work.

The "Overqualified" Problem

If you're applying for roles below your previous level, you'll face the "overqualified" concern. Employers worry you'll leave when something better comes along.

Address this directly: "I know my background might seem like a lot for this role, but I'm excited about [specific aspect of the job/company]. I'm looking for a place where I can contribute immediately while building toward [future goal]."

Show genuine interest in the company and role, not just employment. Research their challenges and explain how your experience helps solve them.

Be realistic about compensation. If you're stepping down in level, you're stepping down in pay too. Don't expect to maintain your previous salary.

Virtual Interview Considerations

Many interviews are still conducted virtually, creating additional challenges when you're unemployed.

Set up in a professional space. Not your bedroom or kitchen. A clean, quiet background shows you're taking this seriously.

Test your technology beforehand. Internet problems or audio issues make you look unprepared, reinforcing negative stereotypes about unemployed candidates.

Dress professionally from head to toe. Even if they can only see your upper body, wearing full professional attire affects your mindset and energy.

Have good lighting and camera positioning. You want to look sharp and engaged, not shadowy or unflattering.

Following Up After Interviews

Unemployed candidates need to follow up strategically. You want to show continued interest without seeming desperate.

Send a thank-you email within 24 hours. Reference specific topics from your conversation and reiterate your interest in the role.

Include any additional information you promised during the interview. This shows follow-through and professionalism.

Wait at least a week before following up again. If they said they'd make a decision by Friday, wait until the following Tuesday to check in.

Keep follow-ups brief and professional. "I wanted to reiterate my interest in the role and see if you need any additional information from me."

Don't follow up more than twice unless they give you a specific reason to do so.

Managing Multiple Interview Processes

If you're lucky enough to have multiple opportunities, manage them carefully.

Be honest about your timeline when asked. "I'm in conversations with a few companies and hoping to make a decision by [date]."

Don't use competing offers as leverage unless you're prepared to walk away. Bluffing rarely works and can backfire.

If you get an offer while waiting to hear from your first choice, ask for a few days to consider it. Then contact your preferred company to let them know you have an offer and ask about their timeline.

Don't string companies along indefinitely. Make decisions in a reasonable timeframe.

When You Don't Get the Job

Rejection stings more when you're unemployed because each "no" feels like another setback. Handle it professionally:

Ask for feedback if the interviewer is open to it. "Is there anything I could have done differently or areas where I should focus my development?"

Stay connected with people who interviewed you. They might think of you for future opportunities or know of openings at other companies.

Don't take rejection personally. There are many reasons jobs go to other candidates that have nothing to do with your qualifications.

Use each interview as practice for the next one. You'll get better at explaining your situation and selling your value.

The Mindset Shift

The biggest challenge of interviewing while unemployed is mental. You feel like you're interviewing from a position of weakness, but that's not true.

You're available to start immediately. That's an advantage over employed candidates who need to give notice.

You've had time to think about what you want next. You're not just looking to escape a bad situation; you're making a thoughtful career move.

You're motivated to succeed. Someone who needs the job is often more committed than someone who's casually exploring options.

Your unemployment is temporary. Focus on your qualifications, experience, and the value you bring. Don't let a temporary status define your entire candidacy.

Remember: they called you for an interview. That means they saw something in your background that interested them. Your job is to remind them why they wanted to talk to you in the first place.

Unemployment makes interviews more stressful, but it doesn't make you less qualified. Prepare well, stay confident, and focus on what you can do for them. The right opportunity is out there.

Negotiating When You Have No Leverage

You got the job offer. After weeks or months of searching, someone finally wants to hire you. You should be celebrating, but instead you're staring at an offer that's lower than you hoped, with benefits that suck, and a start date that feels like surrender.

Now comes the hard part: trying to negotiate when you both know you need this job more than they need you.

Negotiating from unemployment is like playing poker when everyone can see your cards. You're holding a pair of twos, they know it, and they're betting accordingly. You don't have to fold immediately. Even with limited leverage, you can still improve your situation if you're smart about it.

Here's how to negotiate when you have almost no power.

Understanding Your Position

You have less leverage than employed candidates. That's reality. You can't walk away as easily, you can't use competing offers as effectively, and everyone knows you need the money. Pretending otherwise makes you look delusional.

You're not completely powerless. They chose you over other candidates. They invested time in interviews and references. They want you to say yes, not start over with their second choice.

Understanding what leverage you do have and using it strategically beats overplaying a weak hand.

What You Can and Can't Negotiate

Some things are negotiable even when you're unemployed. Others aren't worth fighting over.

You can usually negotiate start dates if you need time to relocate or finish commitments. Titles are sometimes easier to get than salary bumps. Professional development budgets, work-from-home flexibility, vacation time after probationary periods, and review timelines for salary increases are all fair game.

Base salary is harder to negotiate but not impossible. Health insurance contributions, equity at established companies, bonus structures, and perks like parking are tougher sells.

Don't waste time fighting over office supply budgets, conference room booking priority, desk assignments, or company swag. These things don't meaningfully impact your life.

Pick your battles carefully. Don't waste negotiating capital on things that don't matter.

The Salary Conversation

This is where your lack of leverage hurts most. Companies know unemployed people are more likely to accept lower offers.

If the offer is well below market rate, you can push back gently: "I was hoping for something closer to market rate for this role. My research shows similar positions in this area typically range from $X to $Y. Is there flexibility in the salary?"

Don't lie about competing offers unless you have them. "I'm considering other opportunities offering closer to $X" only works if it's true. They might call your bluff.

If they won't budge on base salary, ask about other compensation: "If the base salary isn't flexible, could we discuss a signing bonus or an accelerated review schedule?"

Be prepared to accept their first offer if it's reasonable. When you're unemployed, reasonable beats perfect.

Non-Salary Negotiations

Sometimes it's easier to get non-monetary concessions than salary increases.

Work flexibility is often negotiable: "I'm excited about this opportunity. Would there be flexibility to work from home one or two days a week after the initial training period?"

Professional development budgets can be easier sells: "Could we include a budget for industry conferences or training courses? I'm committed to staying current in this field."

Titles matter for future job searches: "The role sounds like a senior-level position. Would 'Senior Marketing Manager' instead of 'Marketing Manager' be possible?"

Review timelines set expectations for growth: "When would my first performance review be scheduled? I'm hoping to discuss growth opportunities and salary adjustments after I've proven my value."

These requests show you're thinking long-term and invested in success, not just desperate for any job.

Using Time Strategically

Don't accept or reject offers immediately. Even when you're unemployed, you can ask for time to consider.

"Thank you for the offer. I'm excited about the opportunity. Could I have until [day] to review everything and get back to you?"

Use this time to research the company's salary ranges on Glassdoor or similar sites. Think about what concessions would make the offer acceptable. Prepare your negotiation strategy. Check if you have any other interviews that might result in competing offers.

Don't take too long. 24-48 hours is reasonable. A week makes you look indecisive or like you're shopping the offer around.

The Counter-Offer Strategy

If you decide to negotiate, present a clear, reasonable counter-proposal.

"I'm very interested in joining the team. My research and experience level suggest a salary of $X. If that's not possible, would you consider $Y with a review after six months, or perhaps a signing bonus to bridge the gap?"

Give them options. It's easier to say yes to one of three proposals than to negotiate from scratch.

Be prepared for "no." When they say the offer is final, you need to decide: take it or walk away. Don't keep pushing after they've said no twice.

When You Have Competing Offers

If you're lucky enough to have multiple offers, use them carefully.

Don't pit companies against each other in an auction. That works when you have strong leverage, not when you're unemployed.

Use competing offers to establish your value: "I've received another offer for $X. Your opportunity is my preference because of [specific reasons], but the salary difference is significant. Is there any flexibility?"

Be honest about timelines: "I need to respond to the other offer by Friday. Is it possible to finalize our discussion by then?"

Don't fabricate competing offers. It's unethical and they might call your bluff by saying "you should take the other offer."

Handling Lowball Offers

Sometimes companies offer well below market rate, assuming you'll take anything.

Don't get emotional or insulting. "This offer is insulting" kills negotiations.

Present data: "I appreciate the offer. My research shows this role typically pays $X-Y in this market. My experience level usually commands the higher end of that range. Could we discuss the salary?"

If they won't budge, ask why: "Help me understand how you arrived at this number. Is it budget constraints, or is there something about my background that suggests a lower level?"

Sometimes there are legitimate reasons for lower offers: company financial constraints, your experience gaps, or different role scope than you understood.

The "Take It or Leave It" Moment

Eventually, they'll give you their final offer. This is decision time.

Consider the whole package: salary, benefits, growth opportunities, company stability, work environment, commute, industry experience.

Don't just compare to your last job. That job is gone. Compare to your other options, including continued unemployment.

Ask yourself: "Will this job make my life better than it is now? Will it position me well for future opportunities?"

If yes, take it. If no, you need to decide whether to keep looking or accept a stepping-stone position.

Starting Strong Even with a Weak Deal

If you accept a less-than-ideal offer, focus on performing well and positioning for future improvements.

Ask about the review process during negotiation: "When would we discuss performance and potential salary adjustments?"

Document any verbal promises: "Just to confirm, we discussed reviewing my salary after six months based on performance."

Set expectations for growth: "I'm excited to start. What would success look like in this role after the first year?"

Plan your next negotiation from day one. Prove your value, then ask for what you're worth.

What Not to Do

Don't negotiate over email if you can avoid it. Phone calls or video chats allow for real conversation and quick resolution.

Don't bring up personal financial needs: "I really need $X because of my mortgage" isn't persuasive.

Don't threaten to walk away unless you're prepared to do it. Empty threats destroy your credibility.

Don't negotiate every single aspect of the offer. Pick 2-3 things that matter most.

Don't take rejection personally. "We can't do that" isn't an insult, it's just business.

The Long-Term Perspective

Your first job after unemployment won't be your last job. Sometimes you need to take a step back to move forward.

A lower-paying job that gets you back in the workforce might be better than holding out for the perfect offer that never comes.

Focus on roles that give you valuable experience, industry connections, or skills that make you more marketable for the next job.

Build relationships and prove your value. The best time to negotiate is after you've demonstrated results, not before you start.

Making Peace with Compromise

Negotiating from unemployment means accepting less than ideal conditions sometimes. That's not failure, it's strategic thinking.

You're not just taking a job, you're ending unemployment. That has value beyond salary: mental health, professional identity, routine, future opportunities.

Every job is temporary. Even if this one isn't perfect, it can lead to something better.

Focus on what you can control: your performance, your relationships, your skill development. Do those well, and better opportunities will follow.

Negotiating from weakness isn't fun, but it's not impossible. Know what you want, understand what you can get, and make the best deal possible. Sometimes the best deal is just getting back to work.

Starting Your New Job When You're Already Exhausted

You got the job. You start Monday. You should be excited, relieved, ready to prove yourself. Instead, you're emotionally drained, financially stressed, and running on fumes. The months of unemployment have taken their toll, and now you have to show up as your best professional self when you feel like your worst.

This is the cruel irony of unemployment: by the time you find work, you're too beaten down to perform at your peak. You're supposed to make a great first impression when you can barely muster enthusiasm for getting dressed.

You're not broken. You're just tired. Here's how to start strong when you're starting from empty.

The Post-Unemployment Hangover

Unemployment is traumatic, even when it ends well. You've spent weeks or months in rejection, financial stress, and identity crisis. Your confidence is shot. Your routine is nonexistent. Your professional skills feel rusty.

Now you're supposed to flip a switch and become a high-performing employee again. It doesn't work that way.

Give yourself permission to feel exhausted. You've been through something difficult, and it's normal to feel wrung out. Acknowledging this reality helps you manage it better than pretending everything's fine.

You don't have to be perfect on day one. You just have to be present and willing to learn.

Managing Financial Anxiety

Even though you have a job now, the financial anxiety doesn't disappear overnight. You might still be behind on bills, depleted savings, or dealing with debt from your unemployment period.

It takes time for your financial situation to stabilize. Your first paycheck won't fix everything immediately, and that's okay. Make a realistic plan for getting back on track without expecting miracles.

Don't make major financial decisions in your first few months of work. You're still in recovery mode, and big purchases or commitments can wait until you're more stable.

Focus on the basics: paying current expenses, building a small emergency fund, and slowly addressing any debt. The fancy stuff can come later.

Rebuilding Professional Confidence

You might feel like you've forgotten how to work. Imposter syndrome hits hard when you're starting fresh after a period of rejection and self-doubt.

They hired you for a reason. They saw something in your background and interview that convinced them you could do the job. Trust their judgment even if you're questioning your own abilities.

Start small. Focus on doing the basics well before trying to revolutionize anything. Show up on time, ask good questions, complete assignments thoroughly. Build momentum with small wins.

Your skills haven't disappeared. They might be rusty, but they're still there. Give yourself time to remember what you're good at.

Setting Realistic Expectations

You're going to be tired for a while. Job searching is exhausting, and starting a new job requires different energy. Don't expect to be running at full capacity immediately.

Your learning curve will be steeper than usual. When you're stressed and tired, it takes longer to absorb new information and adapt to new environments. That's normal.

Be patient with yourself. Recovery from unemployment takes time, just like recovery from any difficult period. You're not weak for needing time to get back to your best self.

Set small, achievable goals for your first few weeks. Master the coffee machine. Learn everyone's names. Understand the basic workflow. Save the ambitious projects for when you're feeling more grounded.

Building New Routines

Your sleep schedule is a mess. Your eating habits might be off. Your exercise routine has likely disappeared. These basic health factors affect your work performance.

Start rebuilding healthy routines gradually. Go to bed at a reasonable time. Eat regular meals. Take walks. These aren't luxuries, they're professional necessities.

Create structure around your workday. Wake up at the same time, even if you don't need to be at work early. Establish morning and evening routines that help you transition in and out of work mode.

Use your commute time to mentally prepare for and decompress from work. Even if you're working from home, create physical and mental boundaries between work and personal time.

Managing First-Day Nerves

Starting a new job is always nerve-wracking, but it's worse when you're coming from unemployment. You might feel extra pressure to prove yourself immediately.

Everyone expects new employees to need time to get up to speed. You're not supposed to know everything on day one, and asking questions shows engagement, not incompetence.

Prepare the practical stuff in advance. Know where you're going, what time to arrive, what to wear, what to bring. Eliminating uncertainty about logistics helps you focus on the work.

Show up early your first few days. It demonstrates commitment and gives you buffer time to handle any unexpected issues.

Learning the New Environment

Every workplace has its own culture, communication style, and unwritten rules. When you're already overwhelmed, figuring this out can feel impossible.

Watch and listen before trying to make changes or suggestions. Observe how people interact, what the pace feels like, what's considered important. This intelligence gathering helps you adapt faster.

Ask about expectations explicitly. "What does success look like in this role after 90 days?" "How do you prefer to receive updates on my progress?" "What should I prioritize in my first few weeks?"

Find someone who can be an informal mentor or guide. This might be your manager, a colleague, or someone in a similar role. Having a go-to person for questions makes everything easier.

Dealing with Comparison Anxiety

Your new colleagues seem so confident, so settled, so sure of themselves. Meanwhile, you feel like you're faking it. This comparison trap makes everything harder.

Everyone was new once. The person who seems most competent and comfortable felt exactly like you do when they started. Success breeds confidence, not the other way around.

Focus on your own progress, not how you stack up to people who've been there for years. Compare yourself today to yourself last week, not to your colleague who's been there for three years.

Your perspective as an outsider can be valuable. You notice things that longtime employees might miss. Your questions and observations can help the team see blind spots.

When the Job Isn't What You Expected

Sometimes the reality doesn't match what you understood during the interview process. The role might be different, the culture might be off, or the challenges might be bigger than anticipated.

Don't panic immediately. New jobs always involve some adjustment and surprises. Give yourself at least 90 days to get a real sense of whether this is a good fit.

If there are genuine problems, address them professionally. Talk to your manager about role clarity, resource needs, or process improvements. Most issues can be resolved with good communication.

Keep your original goals in mind when evaluating whether it's working. Was it to end unemployment? Gain experience? Enter a new industry? Remember why you took this job.

Building Relationships Carefully

When you're emotionally drained, it's tempting to keep your head down and avoid office social dynamics. But relationships matter for job success and satisfaction.

Start with one or two people instead of trying to connect with everyone immediately. Build a few solid relationships before expanding your network.

Be genuine but professional. You don't need to share your unemployment story or financial struggles with new colleagues. Keep personal information personal until you know people better.

Participate in team activities when you can, but don't force yourself into every social situation. Choose your energy expenditure wisely.

Managing Performance Pressure

You might feel like you need to be exceptional immediately to prove you're worth hiring. This pressure can hurt your performance by creating anxiety and unrealistic expectations.

Consistent good work is better than sporadic brilliance. Focus on being reliable, thorough, and easy to work with. These qualities matter more than occasional flashes of genius.

Ask for feedback regularly. "How am I doing so far?" "Is there anything I should be doing differently?" "What should I focus on improving?" This shows engagement and helps you course-correct quickly.

Document your accomplishments, even small ones. Keep a record of projects completed, problems solved, and positive feedback received. This helps build confidence and prepares you for future performance reviews.

The Long Game

Your first job after unemployment might not be your dream job. That's okay. It's a stepping stone to financial stability and professional re-engagement.

Use this job to rebuild your confidence, update your skills, and expand your network. Even if it's not perfect, it can position you for something better later.

Stay open to opportunities within the company. Sometimes roles evolve, new positions open up, or you discover interests you didn't know you had.

Keep your long-term career goals in mind, but don't sacrifice your current performance for future ambitions. Do well where you are now, and better opportunities will follow.

Taking Care of Yourself

Starting a new job while recovering from unemployment is like running a marathon after being sick. You need to pace yourself and prioritize self-care.

Use your evenings and weekends to recharge, not just catch up on work. Your brain needs downtime to process new information and recover from stress.

Don't skip meals or survive on caffeine. Your body and brain need proper fuel to handle the demands of a new job.

Celebrate small victories. Making it through your first week, completing your first project, getting positive feedback from your manager. These moments matter.

What the First Weeks Actually Look Like

Most people need 3-6 months to feel genuinely settled in a new job, and that timeline is longer when you're coming from unemployment. You won't feel sharp immediately. That's not a problem to solve — it's a timeline to wait out.

Focus on showing up, doing the work in front of you, and not making enemies. That's it for the first month. Ambition can wait until you know where you are.

And start your Always-On Readiness habits from day one — resume current, LinkedIn active, relationships maintained, cash building. Do them now, while you have income and time. The version of you who did that before would not be reading this book.

Making Sure This Never Happens Again

You're back at work. You have a steady paycheck. The immediate crisis is over. The smart thing to do right now is pretend unemployment never happened and go back to your old habits of coasting through your career without a backup plan.

That's exactly what most people do. They get comfortable again, stop networking, let their skills stagnate, and assume their job security is someone else's responsibility. Then they get blindsided by the next layoff, merger, or economic downturn.

You have a choice. You can go back to sleep and hope it never happens again, or you can build a career that's resilient enough to survive whatever comes next. Here's how to make yourself layoff-proof and unemployment-resistant.

The Uncomfortable Truth About Job Security

Job security doesn't exist anymore. It died somewhere between pension plans and the gig economy. The average person will change jobs 12 times during their career, and at least some of those changes won't be voluntary.

Companies don't owe you loyalty, and they've proven they'll eliminate positions whenever it serves their financial interests. The social contract between employers and employees is broken, and it's not getting fixed.

This isn't meant to scare you, it's meant to wake you up. Once you accept that job security is a myth, you can start building real security: the kind that comes from being valuable, connected, and prepared.

Building Financial Resilience

The first line of defense against unemployment is money. Not just an emergency fund, but a robust financial foundation that can weather extended periods without income.

Start with the basics. Build an emergency fund that covers 6-12 months of expenses, not the 3 months that financial advisors used to recommend. In a tough job market, finding work can take longer than you expect.

Reduce your fixed expenses. The less money you need each month to survive, the longer your savings will last and the more flexible you can be about job opportunities. High monthly payments for cars, houses, and lifestyle expenses become anchors when you're unemployed.

Diversify your income streams. This doesn't mean starting a side hustle that makes $50 a month selling crafts online. It means developing skills that can generate real income when your main job disappears: consulting, freelancing, teaching, or contract work in your field.

Keep your skills sharp and marketable. Technology changes, industries evolve, and what made you valuable five years ago might not matter today. Invest in learning new skills before you need them, not after you're laid off.

Career Insurance Through Networking

Your network is your real job security. People hire people they know, trust, and like. If you only network when you need a job, you're too late.

Stay in touch with former colleagues regularly, not just when you're job hunting. Send occasional emails, share interesting articles, congratulate them on promotions, invite them for coffee. These relationships need maintenance.

Attend industry events consistently. Join professional associations. Participate in online communities. The goal isn't collecting business cards, it's building genuine relationships with people in your field.

Help other people before you need help yourself. Make introductions, share job postings, provide advice and insights.

People remember who was generous with their network and who only showed up when they needed something.

Keep your LinkedIn profile updated and active. Share thoughtful content, comment on other people's posts, and stay visible to your professional community. When opportunities arise, you want to be top of mind.

Developing Transferable Skills

Industry knowledge can become obsolete quickly, but transferable skills remain valuable across different roles and companies.

Focus on skills that matter everywhere: project management, data analysis, communication, leadership, problem-solving. These abilities translate across industries and make you valuable in multiple contexts.

Learn to work with different types of people and organizations. Experience with startups, large corporations, nonprofits, and consulting gives you flexibility to pivot when industries contract or change.

Develop expertise in areas that are hard to outsource or automate. Complex problem-solving, strategic thinking, relationship building, and creative work are harder to replace than routine tasks.

Stay current with technology trends in your field. You don't need to become a programmer, but you should understand how technology is changing your industry and what skills will be in demand.

Creating Multiple Career Paths

Don't put all your career eggs in one basket. Develop expertise that opens doors to different types of roles and industries.

If you're in marketing, could you also do business development, sales training, or customer success? If you're in finance, could you move into operations, consulting, or business analysis? Think about adjacent skills that expand your options.

Build a portfolio of accomplishments that tells different stories depending on the audience. Your experience managing budgets could be relevant for finance roles, operations positions, or project management jobs.

Consider roles at different types of organizations. Skills from corporate environments often translate to nonprofits, government, or startups, and vice versa. Don't limit yourself to one sector.

Explore consulting or freelance opportunities in your field. This gives you experience working with different clients, builds your network, and creates potential income streams if your full-time job disappears.

The Early Warning System

Don't wait for a pink slip to start paying attention to your company's financial health and industry trends.

Watch for warning signs at your company: hiring freezes, budget cuts, leadership changes, declining revenue, or talk about "rightsizing" and "efficiency improvements." These often precede layoffs.

Stay informed about your industry. Which companies are struggling? Which are growing? What technologies or business models are disrupting traditional approaches? Understanding these trends helps you position yourself better.

Monitor job market conditions in your field. Are there lots of openings or few? Are salaries rising or stagnating? This information helps you time career moves and understand your leverage.

Keep your resume updated and your skills current even when you're happy in your job. It's easier to make small updates regularly than to rebuild everything when you're under pressure.

The Strategic Job Search

Even when you're employed, you should always be looking. Not applying for jobs, but staying aware of opportunities and maintaining relationships with recruiters.

Take interviews occasionally, even when you're not job hunting. It keeps your interview skills sharp, gives you market intelligence about salaries and opportunities, and maintains relationships with potential employers.

Don't just look at direct competitors. Consider roles at companies that serve your industry, partner with your employer, or operate in adjacent markets. Your skills might be valuable in contexts you haven't considered.

Build relationships with recruiters who specialize in your field. Good recruiters can alert you to opportunities before they're posted publicly and give you insights into market conditions.

Set up job alerts for interesting roles and companies. You don't have to apply for everything, but staying informed about what's available helps you understand your options and market value.

The Side Hustle Reality Check

Not every side hustle is worth your time, but the right ones can provide insurance against unemployment.

Focus on activities that build skills, relationships, or income streams relevant to your main career. Teaching, consulting, or freelancing in your field is more valuable than driving for rideshare companies.

Develop expertise you can monetize independently. Writing, speaking, training, or consulting around your professional knowledge can generate income and build your reputation.

Consider passive income opportunities that don't require constant time investment: rental property, dividend stocks, or digital products that sell while you're doing other things.

Don't let side activities interfere with your main job performance. The goal is insurance, not replacement income. Your primary job should remain your priority.

Building Your Professional Brand

Your reputation and visibility in your industry are assets that provide security across different employers.

Become known for something. Whether it's expertise in a technology, approach to customer service, or ability to turn around struggling teams, having a reputation for value makes you memorable.

Share your knowledge publicly. Write articles, speak at events, participate in industry discussions. This builds your reputation and expands your network beyond your current employer.

Document your accomplishments and impact. Keep records of successful projects, cost savings, revenue generated, or problems solved. This information helps in interviews and salary negotiations.

Get involved in professional organizations and industry initiatives. Serving on committees, organizing events, or contributing to industry publications builds relationships and visibility.

The Long-Term Perspective

Career resilience isn't built overnight. It's the result of consistent effort to build skills, relationships, and financial security.

Make career development an ongoing priority, not something you think about only when changing jobs. Invest time and money in learning, networking, and skill development regularly.

Plan for multiple career scenarios. What would you do if your company was acquired? If your industry contracted? If technology made your role obsolete? Having thought through these possibilities helps you prepare.

Stay curious and adaptable. The careers that thrive are those that evolve with changing conditions. Be willing to learn new things and explore different directions.

Think of unemployment as a temporary setback, not a career catastrophe. With the right preparation, losing a job becomes an inconvenience instead of a crisis.

The Insurance Policy You Control

You can't control when companies lay people off, when industries change, or when economic downturns hit. But you can control how prepared you are when these things happen.

Always-On Readiness

The people who handle job loss best are the ones who were already ready to leave. Not because they were disloyal or had one foot out the door, but because they maintained the habit of readiness as a professional discipline. Always-On Readiness means treating your career like you might need to move tomorrow — while being fully committed to where you are today.

It has four components. First, your resume is never more than 30 days out of date. Every significant project completed, every number you can attach to your work, added while the details are fresh. Second, your LinkedIn profile is active and current — maintained as a living document that reflects who you are right now, not updated in a panic when you need it. Third, you have at least five real professional relationships outside your current employer — people who know your work, not just your name. Fourth, you have three months of expenses in cash, minimum, building toward six.

These aren't signs of disloyalty. They're signs of a professional who understands how employment actually works. Companies maintain contingency plans for every operational risk. You should maintain one for your career. The difference between Always-On Readiness and not having it is the difference between a job loss being a setback and being a catastrophe.

If you had been in Always-On Readiness mode before you picked up this book, your situation right now would be less dire. That's not a criticism — most people aren't. It's a commitment to make before you close it.

The best time to build career insurance is when you don't need it. When you have a job, income, and time to invest in relationships, skills, and financial security.

Start now. Not next month, not when you feel more settled in your new role, not when you have more time. The habits you build today determine how well you weather the next disruption.

Your career is your responsibility. No company, manager, or industry owes you stability. But with the right preparation, you can create your own security and turn future job transitions from crises into opportunities.

The goal isn't to live in fear of unemployment, it's to be so prepared that unemployment becomes manageable. When you know you can survive and thrive regardless of what happens to your current job, you work with confidence instead of anxiety.

That's real job security. The kind you build yourself, control yourself, and carry with you wherever your career goes next.

When to Give Up on Your Old Career

Sometimes the industry is dying, or your skills are obsolete. Sometimes the career you spent decades building is over, and no amount of networking, resume tweaking, or positive thinking will bring it back.

This is the conversation nobody wants to have. Career counselors will tell you to "pivot" or "reinvent yourself." Your family will encourage you to keep trying. You'll read inspiring stories about people who found success after 50 in completely new fields.

Sometimes you need to face reality: your old career is dead, and you need to build a new one.

This isn't failure. This is adaptation. Industries disappear, technology changes everything, and entire categories of work become obsolete. You can either acknowledge this and adapt, or spend years fighting a losing battle.

Here's how to know when it's time to give up on your old career and what to do next.

Signs Your Industry Is Dying

Some industries die slowly, others collapse overnight. If you're in newspapers, retail, or coal mining, the writing has been on the wall for years. If you're in travel, hospitality, or traditional banking, recent changes might have accelerated existing trends.

Look at job postings in your field. Are there fewer positions than there were five years ago? Are the salaries declining? Are companies requiring different skills than they used to?

Check industry publications and trade associations. Are they talking about "transformation" and "disruption" constantly? Are veteran professionals leaving for other industries? Are conferences getting smaller?

Talk to recruiters who specialize in your field. Are they busy, or are they pivoting to other industries? What are they telling candidates about market conditions?

Look at where the money is going. If investment is flowing out of your industry instead of into it, that's a clear signal. If companies are cutting R&D and capital expenditures, they're managing decline, not planning growth.

Signs Your Skills Are Obsolete

Sometimes the industry survives but your role within it doesn't. Technology eliminates jobs, changes required skills, or makes entire departments unnecessary.

Look at job descriptions for roles similar to yours. Do they require skills you don't have? Are they asking for experience with tools or platforms that didn't exist when you started your career?

Notice what younger people in your field are doing differently. Are they using different software, following different processes, or focusing on different metrics? If there's a growing gap between your approach and theirs, that's a warning sign.

Check salary trends for your role. If compensation is declining or stagnating while other roles in the same company are growing, your function might be losing importance.

Ask yourself honestly: could your job be automated, outsourced, or eliminated without hurting the business? If the answer is yes, it probably will be.

The Sunk Cost Trap

You've invested years or decades building expertise in your field. You have a reputation, relationships, and knowledge that took time to develop. Starting over feels like throwing that all away.

This is the sunk cost fallacy. The time and effort you've already invested doesn't justify continuing to invest in something that's no longer viable. Your past investment is gone regardless of what you do next.

Think about it this way: would you spend the next five years trying to resurrect a dead career, or building a new one that has a future?

Your experience isn't worthless, even if your role is obsolete. Skills transfer across industries, relationships can be valuable in new contexts, and the general business knowledge you've gained still matters.

The Emotional Reality

Giving up on your career identity is hard. If you've been a journalist for 20 years, admitting that journalism is dying feels like admitting that you wasted your life.

You didn't waste your life. You had a career during the time when that career made sense. Now the world has changed, and you need to change with it.

Allow yourself to grieve. It's normal to feel angry, sad, or scared about starting over. These feelings are valid and necessary. Don't try to skip past them with forced optimism.

Don't get stuck in them either. Grief has a purpose, but it's not a permanent state. At some point, you need to stop mourning what's gone and start building what's next.

Transferable Assets

Even if your career is dead, you have assets that transfer to new opportunities.

Industry knowledge: Understanding how businesses work, what customers want, and what problems need solving is valuable across many fields.

Professional network: People you've worked with might be in different industries now or might know opportunities outside your original field.

General business skills: Project management, budgeting, leadership, communication, problem-solving. These matter everywhere.

Work ethic and professionalism: Knowing how to show up, meet deadlines, work with others, and handle responsibility. These basics are always in demand.

Life experience: Understanding how the world works, how to navigate complex situations, and how to learn new things quickly. This wisdom has value.

Choosing Your Next Direction

Don't just jump into the first alternative you find. Be strategic about what you do next.

Look for growing industries that need people with your background. Healthcare, technology, renewable energy, and elder care are expanding. Where could your experience be valuable?

Consider adjacent fields where your knowledge applies differently. If you were in print journalism, could you do content marketing? If you were in retail management, could you do logistics or e-commerce?

Think about problems you could solve. What frustrates you about products or services you use? What inefficiencies do you notice in businesses you interact with? Sometimes the best opportunities come from applying your experience to new problems.

Look at demographic trends. An aging population creates opportunities in healthcare, financial planning, and lifestyle services. Remote work creates needs for collaboration tools and home office services.

The Reality of Starting Over

Starting a new career later in life is challenging but not impossible. You're competing with younger people who might work for less money and longer hours. You're learning new skills while they grew up with them.

You also have advantages. You understand business in ways that 25-year-olds don't. You have perspective, judgment, and patience. You know how to work with difficult people and handle stressful situations.

Be realistic about the timeline. Building expertise in a new field takes years, not months. Your first role in a new industry might not pay what you used to make or carry the same status you once had.

Think of this as a long-term investment. Taking a step back now to learn new skills and build new relationships can lead to better opportunities later.

Practical Steps

Start by researching your target industry extensively. Read trade publications, follow industry leaders on social media, attend virtual conferences. Understand the language, trends, and key players.

Identify the skills you need and start building them. Take online courses, get certifications, volunteer for projects that give you relevant experience. Don't wait until you're job-ready to start learning.

Begin networking in your new field before you need a job. Join professional associations, attend meetups, participate in online communities. Build relationships while you're still employed if possible.

Consider transitional roles that bridge your old career and your new one. Consulting in your original field while building skills in your target area. Contract work that gives you flexibility to learn and explore.

Update all your professional materials to reflect your new direction. LinkedIn profile, resume, elevator pitch. Start presenting yourself as someone moving toward your new field, not someone stuck in the old one.

When to Make the Jump

Don't wait until your old career is completely dead to start building a new one. The best time to change careers is when you still have options, not when you're desperate.

If you see the writing on the wall, start preparing now. Build skills, make connections, and position yourself for the transition while you still have income and stability.

Don't wait forever either. Analysis paralysis can keep you stuck in a dying field while opportunities in new areas pass you by.

Set a timeline. Give yourself six months to explore and prepare, then start pursuing opportunities in your new field. Having a deadline creates urgency and prevents endless preparation without action.

The Success Stories Are Real

You'll read about people who successfully changed careers later in life, and you might dismiss them as exceptions or luck. Some of them are, but many are people who recognized reality and adapted to it.

The teacher who became a software developer. The newspaper editor who became a digital marketing consultant. The retail manager who became a logistics coordinator. These transitions happen, but they require acknowledging that the old path is closed and committing to a new one.

Your story could be one of those success stories, but only if you're willing to let go of what isn't working and build something new.

The Alternative

The alternative to changing careers is staying in a field that's shrinking or eliminating your role. You can keep applying for fewer and fewer jobs, watching your skills become more obsolete, and hoping that things will somehow return to how they used to be.

They won't. The world doesn't move backward. Industries that are dying today will be more dead tomorrow. Skills that are obsolete now will be more obsolete next year.

You can spend the next decade of your career fighting this reality, or you can spend it building something new.

Making Peace with Change

Career change later in life isn't what you planned. You thought you'd continue growing in your field, maybe become a senior expert or leader, then retire with a sense of accomplishment and expertise.

That narrative is broken now, and you need to write a new one. The new story might be better than the old one, but it will be different.

Success in your fifties or sixties might look different than success in your thirties or forties. It might mean finding work that's meaningful instead of prestigious, stable instead of exciting, or flexible instead of high-paying.

That's not settling. That's evolving. The goals that made sense earlier in your career might not make sense now, and that's okay.

Your career isn't over just because your old career is dead. You're not too old to learn new things, meet new people, or find new opportunities. You just need to stop looking backward and start looking forward.

The next chapter of your career is waiting to be written. First, you have to close the book on the last one.

Unemployment and Disability

If you're dealing with unemployment while managing a disability, you're facing challenges that most job search advice doesn't address. Should you disclose your disability to employers? How do you ask for accommodations without seeming like a burden? What happens to your benefits if you start working?

The reality is that people with disabilities face higher unemployment rates and additional barriers that go beyond the standard job search frustrations. Employers often have misconceptions about disability and work capacity. The legal protections exist on paper, but discrimination still happens in subtle ways that are hard to prove.

This chapter addresses the practical realities of job searching with a disability, from deciding whether to disclose to navigating benefits systems to finding employers who follow through on their inclusion commitments.

The Disclosure Dilemma

The biggest question most people with disabilities face during job searching is whether and when to disclose their disability. There's no universal right answer because it depends on your situation, your disability, and your local job market.

If you have a visible disability, disclosure isn't really a choice. You'll need to address it proactively instead of hoping employers won't notice or ask questions. Frame your disability matter-of-factly and quickly pivot to your qualifications and what accommodations, if any, you might need.

If you have an invisible disability, you have more options but also more anxiety about the decision. Chronic illnesses, mental health conditions, learning disabilities, and many other conditions aren't apparent to employers unless you choose to reveal them.

Early disclosure filters out discriminatory employers before you waste time in their hiring process. If a company is going to have problems with your disability, you want to know that before you invest hours in interviews and applications. Early disclosure also allows you to request interview accommodations if needed.

The case against early disclosure is that it can trigger unconscious bias before employers get to know your qualifications. Even well-meaning hiring managers might make assumptions about your capabilities or the cost and complexity of accommodations. You might be eliminated from consideration before getting a chance to demonstrate your abilities.

Many people choose a middle path: they don't disclose during the application phase but bring it up after receiving a job offer. This approach lets you get through the initial screening based on your qualifications alone, but still allows you to negotiate accommodations before starting work.

There's no perfect strategy, and what works depends on your industry, local culture, and personal comfort level. The key is making a deliberate choice instead of avoiding the decision until it's forced on you.

Understanding Your Legal Rights

The Americans with Disabilities Act requires employers with 15 or more employees to provide reasonable accommodations for qualified people with disabilities. Understanding what this means in practice helps you navigate the job search and workplace accommodation process.

You're protected if you have a physical or mental impairment that substantially limits one or more major life activities. This covers obvious conditions like mobility impairments and blindness, but also less visible conditions like diabetes, depression, ADHD, and chronic pain.

Reasonable accommodations are modifications to the job or workplace that allow you to perform the essential functions of the position. Common accommodations include flexible schedules, modified equipment, remote work options, reserved parking spaces, and adjusted break schedules.

Employers don't have to provide accommodations that create an "undue hardship," which generally means excessive cost or operational difficulty relative to the size and resources of the business. They also don't have to eliminate essential job functions or create new positions.

The accommodation process is supposed to be an interactive dialogue between you and the employer. You request an accommodation, provide medical documentation if needed, and work together to find solutions that meet your needs while allowing you to do the job effectively.

The reality is more complicated than the legal framework suggests. Many employers don't understand their obligations under the ADA. Some resist providing accommodations even when they're required to do so. Others make assumptions about what accommodations will cost or how disruptive they'll be without investigating options.

Discrimination still happens, but it's often subtle. You might not get called for interviews after disclosing a disability. You might be asked illegal questions about your medical condition. You might be told you're "not a good fit" for vague reasons that seem related to your disability.

Navigating the Application Process

Applying for jobs with a disability requires some strategic thinking about how and when to present information about your condition and accommodation needs.

Most job applications include a voluntary disclosure section asking if you have a disability. This information is supposed to be used only for affirmative action tracking and shouldn't influence hiring decisions. In practice, some employers might use this information inappropriately, but others genuinely use it only for reporting purposes.

Deciding whether to check the disability box depends on your risk tolerance and the employer. Government agencies and large corporations with strong compliance programs are generally safer bets for voluntary disclosure than small businesses with less HR infrastructure.

If you choose not to disclose during the application phase, focus on highlighting your qualifications and achievements without mentioning disability-related gaps or accommodations. Your goal is to get to the interview stage based on your merits.

If you do disclose early, consider including a brief statement about your ability to perform the job with or without reasonable accommodations. This proactive approach can address concerns before they become barriers: "I have a visual impairment and use screen-reading software, which doesn't affect my ability to perform accounting functions."

Resume gaps related to disability can be challenging to explain. Extended medical leaves, time spent in treatment, or periods when your condition was unmanaged might create employment gaps that require explanation. Consider using years instead of months on your resume to minimize apparent gaps, or briefly explain periods of health management in your cover letter.

Interview Strategies and Accommodations

Job interviews can be stressful when you're managing disclosure decisions and potential accommodation needs. Preparation is crucial for handling these situations confidently.

If you disclosed your disability during the application process, be prepared for questions about accommodations and job performance. Practice explaining your condition briefly and matter-of-factly, then quickly shift focus to your qualifications and experience.

If you haven't disclosed yet, decide before the interview whether you'll bring it up during the conversation or wait until after receiving an offer. There's no requirement to disclose during interviews unless your disability affects your ability to perform essential job functions even with accommodations.

Employers can't legally ask about your medical condition, but they can ask if you need accommodations for the interview process. If you need a wheelchair-accessible location, sign language interpreter, extended time, or other modifications, request these when scheduling the interview.

During the interview, focus on your qualifications and experience instead of spending excessive time on disability-related topics. Answer accommodation questions honestly but briefly: "Yes, I use a mobility aid, but it doesn't affect my ability to perform the essential functions of this position."

Be prepared to address concerns that employers might have but can't directly ask about. If your disability might affect attendance, mention your reliability record. If it might impact certain tasks, explain how you accomplish those functions or what accommodations would help.

The goal is to present yourself as a qualified candidate who happens to have a disability, not as a disabled person who might be able to do the job. Confidence and focus on your professional capabilities help employers see past their misconceptions about disability.

Accommodation Conversations

Requesting workplace accommodations can feel intimidating, especially if you're worried about being seen as high-maintenance or expensive. Understanding the process and preparing your requests helps these conversations go more smoothly.

Start by researching what accommodations might be helpful for your situation and job requirements. The Job Accommodation Network provides free resources about accommodations for different conditions and industries. Knowing what's possible helps you make informed requests.

When requesting accommodations, be clear about what you need and how it will help you perform your job duties. "I need a quiet workspace" is less helpful than "I need a workspace away from high-traffic areas because my ADHD makes it difficult to concentrate with frequent interruptions."

Come prepared with information about costs and implementation. Many accommodations cost little or nothing to implement. Remote work options, flexible schedules, and modified break periods don't require equipment purchases. Even assistive technology is often less expensive than employers expect.

Be willing to engage in the interactive process. Your first suggestion might not work for operational reasons, but there might be alternative solutions that meet both your needs and the employer's constraints. Flexibility and problem-solving demonstrate that you're a collaborative employee.

Document accommodation requests and responses in writing. Email summaries of verbal conversations help create a paper trail if issues arise later. This documentation also helps ensure that accommodation agreements survive management changes or departmental reorganizations.

Benefits and Work Considerations

Returning to work while receiving disability benefits involves complex rules that vary depending on which programs you're receiving. Understanding these rules helps you make informed decisions about job opportunities and work arrangements.

Social Security Disability Insurance has work incentive programs that allow you to test your ability to work while maintaining benefit protections. The Trial Work Period lets you work for nine months while still receiving full benefits, regardless of how much you earn during those months.

After the trial work period, you enter the Extended Period of Eligibility, where you only receive benefits for months when your earnings fall below substantial gainful activity levels.

Currently, that's about $1,500 per month for most people, though the amount changes annually.

Supplemental Security Income has different rules about work and earnings. Any earned income reduces your SSI payment, but you can usually keep more money overall by working part-time than by relying solely on benefits.

Medicaid coverage through disability programs can continue even when you return to work, depending on your state's rules. Some states have Medicaid Buy-In programs that allow people with disabilities to work and pay a premium to maintain Medicaid coverage.

The key is understanding these rules before you start working so you can make informed decisions about job offers and work arrangements. Social Security's Work Incentives Planning and Assistance programs provide free counseling about how work affects benefits.

Finding Disability-Friendly Employers

Not all employers are equally committed to disability inclusion, despite legal requirements. Some companies go beyond compliance to create genuinely inclusive workplaces, while others do the minimum required by law. Targeting disability-friendly employers can improve your job search success.

Large corporations often have more resources for accommodations and stronger compliance programs. They're also more likely to have employee resource groups for people with disabilities and structured diversity and inclusion initiatives.

Government agencies are generally good options because they're subject to stricter accessibility requirements and often have explicit diversity goals that include disability representation.

Nonprofit organizations, especially those serving people with disabilities, tend to be more understanding of accommodation needs and disability-related workplace issues.

Some companies participate in disability employment initiatives like the National Organization on Disability's Corporate Leadership Council or the U.S. Business Leadership Network. These organizations indicate a commitment to disability inclusion beyond basic legal compliance.

Research potential employers' accessibility and inclusion track records before applying. Look for accessibility statements on their websites, employee testimonials about accommodation experiences, and participation in disability employment programs.

Managing Invisible Disabilities

Invisible disabilities like chronic illnesses, mental health conditions, learning differences, and chronic pain present unique challenges in the workplace and job search process.

The advantage of invisible disabilities is that you have more control over disclosure timing and can establish your professional credibility before addressing accommodation needs. The disadvantage is that your needs might be less understood or taken seriously than those of people with visible disabilities.

Energy management becomes crucial when you have conditions that cause fatigue, pain, or cognitive fog. Plan your job search activities during times when you typically feel better. Don't schedule multiple interviews on the same day if that's likely to exhaust you.

Be honest with yourself about what work arrangements you need to be successful. If you need flexible start times because of medication effects, morning stiffness, or medical appointments, look for jobs that can accommodate schedule flexibility.

Consider remote work options if commuting or office environments exacerbate your condition. The expansion of remote work since COVID-19 has created more opportunities for people whose disabilities are better managed from home.

Prepare explanations for productivity variations that might be noticed by supervisors. "I have a medical condition that sometimes affects my energy levels, but I consistently meet my deadlines by managing my workload strategically" can address concerns while maintaining privacy.

Mental Health and Employment

Mental health conditions are covered under the ADA, but stigma around mental illness can make disclosure decisions difficult. Employers might have more misconceptions about mental health conditions than about physical disabilities.

Common accommodations for mental health conditions include flexible schedules, modified break periods, quiet workspaces, written instructions instead of verbal ones, and remote work options. Many of these accommodations benefit all employees, not just those with mental health conditions.

If you're managing depression, anxiety, PTSD, or other mental health conditions, consider how work stress might affect your symptoms. Jobs with high pressure, irregular schedules, or toxic workplace cultures can exacerbate mental health problems.

Be realistic about your stress tolerance and work capacity while also challenging yourself appropriately. Underemployment can be as problematic as overextending yourself if it leads to financial stress or lack of professional fulfillment.

Consider whether employee assistance programs, health insurance mental health coverage, and workplace wellness initiatives are important factors in your job search. Employers with strong mental health support systems might be better fits for your long-term success.

Technology and Accessibility

Assistive technology has made many jobs more accessible for people with disabilities, but not all employers understand what's available or how to implement these solutions effectively.

If you use assistive technology, research compatibility with common workplace software and systems. Being able to say "I use JAWS screen reader, which is compatible with your Microsoft Office suite" demonstrates that you've thought through implementation details.

Many accommodations involve software instead of expensive hardware purchases. Voice recognition software, screen magnifiers, and cognitive assistance apps are relatively inexpensive solutions that can address a wide range of accommodation needs.

Remote work technology has expanded opportunities for people whose disabilities make traditional office environments challenging. Video conferencing, cloud-based collaboration tools, and digital project management systems can support flexible work arrangements.

Be prepared to provide guidance about assistive technology implementation if you're the first employee with certain accommodation needs. Your expertise can help employers understand that technology solutions are often simpler and less expensive than they assume.

Self-Advocacy and Professional Development

Successfully managing a career with a disability requires ongoing self-advocacy skills and attention to professional development opportunities that support your long-term goals.

Learn to communicate your needs clearly and confidently. Practice explaining your accommodation requests in terms of job performance instead of medical necessity. "I need a height-adjustable desk to perform computer work effectively" is more compelling than "I have back problems."

Stay current with developments in your field and in disability rights and accommodations. New assistive technologies, legal precedents, and workplace inclusion practices can create opportunities that didn't exist when you first entered the workforce.

Connect with other professionals with disabilities in your industry. Professional associations often have disability-focused networking groups that provide career support, mentorship, and job leads from employers who value disability inclusion.

Consider whether becoming visible as a person with a disability in your professional community aligns with your career goals. Some people find that disability advocacy and consulting become valuable additions to their professional expertise.

Long-term Career Planning

Disability can affect career planning in ways that require strategic thinking about job choices, skill development, and financial planning.

Consider how your condition might change and how that could affect your work capacity or accommodation needs. Progressive conditions might require thinking about career transitions before they become necessary.

Build portable skills that aren't dependent on work environments or physical capabilities. Technology skills, communication abilities, and industry knowledge can transfer across different jobs and accommodation scenarios.

Develop multiple income streams if possible. Freelance work, consulting, or passive income sources can provide financial security if your disability affects your ability to maintain traditional full-time employment.

Plan for potential periods of reduced work capacity by building emergency funds and understanding your benefit options.

Knowing what supports are available reduces anxiety about health changes that might affect your employment.

Moving Forward

Job searching with a disability requires balancing honesty about your needs with strategic presentation of your qualifications. The goal isn't to hide your disability, but to ensure that employers see your professional capabilities alongside your accommodation needs.

The employment landscape for people with disabilities is slowly improving as employers recognize the value of inclusive workplaces and assistive technology makes more jobs accessible. Your success contributes to broader changes that benefit other people with disabilities.

Focus on finding employers who see disability inclusion as a business advantage instead of a compliance burden. These organizations are more likely to provide meaningful accommodations and advancement opportunities.

Your disability is one aspect of your professional identity, not the defining characteristic. You bring skills, experience, and perspectives that have value beyond any accommodations you might need.

The right job exists for you. It might take longer to find it, and you might need to be more strategic about your search, but meaningful employment is possible for people with disabilities who approach the process thoughtfully and persistently.

Finding Work After Retirement

Retirement was supposed to be the reward for 40 years of work. You were supposed to relax, travel, pursue hobbies, and enjoy your golden years. Instead, you're reading a book about finding employment because retirement isn't working out the way you planned.

Maybe your savings weren't enough. Maybe healthcare costs are higher than expected. Maybe inflation ate into your fixed income. Maybe you're just bored out of your mind and need something to do. Whatever brought you here, you're facing a job market that's changed dramatically since the last time you looked for work.

You're also dealing with age discrimination that's real, widespread, and mostly legal. Employers will find creative ways to avoid hiring you that have nothing to do with your qualifications and everything to do with your age. This chapter will help you navigate those challenges and find work that fits your situation.

Why Retirees Return to Work

The reasons people go back to work after retirement usually fall into three categories: money, boredom, or benefits.

Money is the most common reason. You discovered that Social Security and your savings don't cover your expenses. Healthcare costs are higher than you budgeted for. Your pension is smaller than expected, or your 401(k) took a hit in the market. Inflation has made everything more expensive while your income stays fixed.

Boredom is more common than people admit. Retirement sounds great when you're working 50-hour weeks, but the reality of having nothing to do can be depressing. You miss having purpose, structure, and social interaction. You miss feeling useful and productive.

Benefits drive some people back to work, especially healthcare. If you retire before 65 and lose employer coverage, individual health insurance can cost more than rent. Even after Medicare kicks in, supplemental coverage and prescription costs can be substantial.

None of these reasons are shameful or unusual. The retirement system assumes people have substantial savings, low healthcare costs, and the ability to live on reduced income. That's not reality for most people.

The Age Discrimination Reality

Let's address the elephant in the room: employers don't want to hire older workers. They worry you're too expensive, too set in your ways, too likely to have health problems, or too close to leaving again. Some think you can't learn new technology or adapt to change.

These stereotypes are mostly wrong, but they affect hiring decisions anyway. The law prohibits age discrimination, but it's almost impossible to prove. Employers will find other reasons not to hire you: "overqualified," "not a good cultural fit," "looking for someone with different experience."

You can't eliminate age bias, but you can work around it. The goal isn't to hide your age (that's obvious from your work history), but to present yourself as current, flexible, and motivated.

What You Have That Younger Workers Don't

Stop focusing on your disadvantages and start leveraging your advantages. You have things that younger workers don't, and some employers value these qualities.

You have experience. You've seen economic cycles, management changes, and industry transformations. You know how to handle crises because you've handled them before. You have institutional knowledge that can't be taught.

You have work ethic. You show up on time, you do what you say you'll do, and you don't call in sick because you're hungover. You're not constantly checking your phone or looking for the next opportunity. Employers appreciate reliability.

You have perspective. You're not trying to climb the corporate ladder or prove yourself. You can focus on getting the work done without the drama and politics that often come with ambitious younger employees.

You have flexibility. You don't need traditional career advancement or high salaries. You might be willing to work part-time, seasonal, or temporary positions that don't appeal to people building careers.

You have time. You're not juggling small children, soccer practices, and school events. You can work evenings, weekends, or holidays when needed.

Types of Work That Suit Retirees

Not all jobs are equally welcoming to older workers. Some industries and roles are more age-friendly than others.

Customer service roles often work well because employers value maturity and life experience when dealing with difficult customers. Retail positions, especially at higher-end stores, appreciate older workers who can relate to their customer base.

Consulting in your former field lets you leverage decades of experience. Companies need expertise for specific projects but don't want full-time employees. Your age becomes an asset because it implies deep knowledge.

Part-time and seasonal work suits many retirees' schedules and income needs. Tax preparation, retail holiday help, summer camp counseling, and tutoring offer flexible schedules without long-term commitments.

Administrative and support roles in healthcare, education, and nonprofits often value mature workers. These organizations serve older populations and appreciate employees who can relate to their clients.

Education and training roles let you share your expertise. Substitute teaching, corporate training, and community college instruction can be rewarding ways to stay engaged.

Updating Your Approach

If you haven't job searched in years or decades, the process has changed. Applications are mostly online now. Networking happens through LinkedIn and email, not just golf courses and cocktail parties. Interviews might be conducted over video calls.

Your resume needs updating beyond just adding recent experience. The format, language, and focus have all evolved. Remove graduation dates and early career experience that dates you. Focus on recent accomplishments and current skills.

Learn basic technology if you haven't already. You need to be comfortable with email, online applications, and video calls. You don't need to be an expert, but you can't be completely helpless with technology.

Update your professional image. Your LinkedIn profile photo shouldn't be from 1995. Your email address shouldn't be "grampajoe@aol.com." Small things like this unconsciously bias people against you.

The Part-Time Advantage

Many retirees prefer part-time work, and this can be an advantage in your job search. Employers often struggle to fill part-time positions because career-focused workers want full-time jobs with benefits.

You can be selective about part-time opportunities because you're not dependent on them for full benefits. You might already have Medicare and Social Security, so you don't need employer healthcare and retirement contributions.

Part-time work also lets you test employers and industries without major commitments. If a job doesn't work out, you can leave without the financial stress that younger workers would face.

Be honest about your part-time preference in interviews. Don't pretend you want full-time work if you don't. Employers appreciate honesty about schedule preferences and availability.

Addressing the Retirement Question

Interviewers will ask why you want to work instead of enjoying retirement. This question can feel invasive, but it's coming from legitimate concerns about your motivation and longevity.

Have a clear, honest answer ready. If you need the income, say so directly: "Healthcare costs are higher than I budgeted for, and I need to supplement my retirement income." If you're bored, explain it positively: "I miss the challenge and social interaction of work."

Don't apologize for wanting to work. Frame it as a choice, not desperation. "I have the luxury of being selective about opportunities, and this role appeals to me because..."

Address concerns about longevity directly. If you're planning to work for several years, say so. If you're looking for seasonal or project-based work, explain that upfront.

Salary Negotiations for Retirees

Your salary negotiation position is different from younger workers. You might be willing to accept lower pay in exchange for flexibility, interesting work, or reduced stress. You might also have more freedom to walk away from offers that don't meet your needs.

Don't accept low-ball offers just because you're older. Your experience has value, and you shouldn't work for poverty wages unless that's your only option.

Consider the total compensation package, not just salary. Healthcare benefits, flexible schedules, vacation time, and professional development might matter more to you than they would to someone building a career.

Be prepared to negotiate non-traditional arrangements. Remote work, flexible hours, or compressed schedules might be more valuable to you than extra money.

When Your Industry Has Changed

If you're returning to your former field after years of retirement, you might discover that your industry has evolved. Technology, regulations, best practices, and business models may have changed.

Don't pretend you're current if you're not. Acknowledge that you've been out of the field but emphasize your foundation knowledge and willingness to learn. "The software has changed, but the underlying principles of accounting haven't."

Consider taking a refresher course or earning a current certification. Community colleges and professional associations often offer update courses designed for returning workers.

Look for bridge opportunities that let you get current gradually. Temporary assignments, consulting projects, or part-time roles can help you rebuild your knowledge and confidence.

The Overqualification Problem

You'll frequently be told you're "overqualified" for positions. This is often code for "too old" or "too expensive," but sometimes it's a legitimate concern that you'll be bored and leave quickly.

Address overqualification concerns directly. Explain why the role interests you despite being below your previous level. "I'm looking for less stress and more work-life balance" or "I want to focus on direct service instead of management."

Consider removing some experience from your resume if it makes you seem overqualified for positions you want. You don't have to list every job you've ever had if it hurts your chances of getting interviews.

Be prepared to discuss why you're willing to take a step back in responsibility or compensation. Have reasons beyond "I need a job."

Finding Age-Friendly Employers

Some employers are more welcoming to older workers than others. Target your search toward companies and industries known for valuing experience and maturity.

Nonprofits often appreciate older volunteers and employees, especially those serving senior populations. Healthcare organizations value mature workers who can relate to older patients.

Government positions typically have stronger anti-discrimination protections and formal hiring processes that reduce bias. Many government agencies recruit older workers.

Small businesses sometimes prefer older employees because they appreciate reliability and don't expect rapid advancement or high salaries.

Research company demographics before applying. If everyone in their marketing materials looks like they're 25, they might not be an age-friendly employer.

Networking in Retirement

Your professional network from your working years is still valuable, even if some contacts have also retired. Former colleagues can provide references, job leads, and industry insights.

Professional associations often have emeritus or retired member categories that keep you connected to your field. Attend meetings and events to stay current and visible.

Community involvement can lead to work opportunities. Volunteering, serving on boards, or participating in civic organizations puts you in contact with people who might need your skills.

Don't overlook informal networks. Your neighbors, friends, and family might know about opportunities that would be perfect for someone in your situation.

The Technology Challenge

If you're uncomfortable with technology, you need to address this before you start job searching. You don't need to be an expert, but you need basic competency.

Learn essential applications like email, Microsoft Office or Google Workspace, and video calling software like Zoom. These are minimum requirements for most office work.

Practice online job applications before you need them. Many systems are poorly designed and confusing, so it helps to be familiar with the process.

Consider taking a computer class at your local library or community college. Many offer sessions designed for older adults.

Ask younger family members or friends for help if you're struggling. Most people are happy to teach basic computer skills to someone who's genuinely trying to learn.

Managing Expectations

Your second career won't look like your first one. You might not get the same level of responsibility, salary, or respect that you had before retirement. This isn't necessarily bad, but it requires adjusting your expectations.

You're not competing with 30-year-olds for promotions and corner offices. You're looking for work that provides income, purpose, and social interaction on terms that work for your life stage.

Success might mean finding a part-time job you enjoy instead of a high-powered executive position. It might mean working seasonally instead of year-round. Define success based on your current needs, not your past achievements.

The Financial Considerations

Working after retirement affects your Social Security benefits, Medicare coverage, and tax situation. Understand these implications before you start working.

If you're receiving Social Security before full retirement age, there are limits on how much you can earn without reducing your benefits. Once you reach full retirement age, these limits disappear.

Working might affect your Medicare premiums if your income exceeds certain thresholds. Factor this into your salary negotiations and job decisions.

Consider how employment income affects your overall tax situation. You might need to make quarterly payments or adjust withholdings to avoid penalties.

Consult a financial advisor or tax professional if you're unsure about how employment will affect your retirement benefits and taxes.

The Social Aspect

Don't underestimate the social benefits of working after retirement. Many retirees miss the daily interaction with colleagues and the sense of being part of a team.

Work provides structure and purpose that can be hard to create on your own. Having somewhere to go and something to do can improve your mental health and overall well-being.

You'll meet new people and develop friendships with coworkers of different ages. This can be energizing and help combat the isolation that many retirees experience.

Making Peace with Starting Over

Starting over in your 60s or 70s feels different from starting over in your 20s or 30s. You might feel like you're going backward or that your previous accomplishments don't matter.

You're not starting from zero. You have decades of experience, skills, and knowledge that have value. You're adding to your career, not replacing it.

This phase of work can be more enjoyable than your primary career because you have less pressure and more freedom. You can choose opportunities based on interest instead of advancement potential.

The Long View

Working after retirement might be temporary or permanent, depending on your circumstances and preferences. Some people work for a few years to improve their financial situation, then retire again. Others discover they enjoy working and continue indefinitely.

Stay flexible about your plans. Your health, financial situation, and interests might change. What works now might not work in five years, and that's okay.

Consider this an experiment instead of a permanent commitment. If a job doesn't work out, you can try something else or stop working altogether. You have more freedom to make changes than someone who depends entirely on employment income.

Moving Forward

Looking for work after retirement requires adapting your approach to current realities while leveraging the advantages that come with your age and experience. You're not the same person who entered the workforce decades ago, and that's a good thing.

You have perspective, patience, and skills that come only with experience. You also have the freedom to be selective in ways that younger workers don't. Use these advantages strategically while addressing the challenges honestly.

The job market has changed, but opportunities exist for older workers who approach their search thoughtfully. You might not get your dream job, but you can find work that provides income, purpose, and satisfaction during this phase of your life.

Your working years don't have to end when you thought they would. Sometimes the most rewarding work comes later in life when you're free from the pressure to climb ladders and prove yourself. This could be the most enjoyable chapter of your career.

Don't Get Scammed When You're Desperate

The email looked legitimate. "Congratulations! We've reviewed your resume and would like to offer you a position as a Customer Service Representative with our company. Starting salary \$22/hour, work from home, flexible schedule. Please confirm your interest by replying with your full name, address, and Social Security number for our HR department."

You've been unemployed for four months. Your savings are almost gone, and your landlord is asking about next month's rent. Twenty-two dollars an hour sounds amazing for a work-from-home job, especially since you've been applying to customer service positions paying half that much.

You almost hit reply. Then you notice the email came from a Gmail account, not a company domain. The sender's name is "HRDepartment2023," which seems odd. You Google the company name and find a website that looks professional but has no physical address or phone number.

You didn't fall for it. Thousands of unemployed people do every day. When you're desperate, your judgment gets cloudy. You want to believe that someone values your skills enough to offer you good money for easy work. Scammers know this, and they design their schemes to exploit that desperation.

How These Scams Actually Work

Here's how sophisticated these operations have become. Scammers don't post obvious fake ads anymore. They research real companies, copy legitimate job postings, and create convincing impostors. They use real company logos, real benefit descriptions, and real-sounding HR department names.

The goal isn't always to steal money directly. Often it's collecting personal information — Social Security numbers, bank account details for "payroll setup" — from people desperate enough to hand it over before verifying anything is real.

Companies whose identities get hijacked this way end up fielding calls from people who believe they've been hired — asking why their equipment hasn't arrived, why the onboarding portal doesn't work. Some of those people have already handed over everything the scammer needed.

The Anatomy of Desperation

When you're unemployed and running out of money, you become a different version of yourself. You're more trusting, more hopeful, and more willing to take risks. You check your email obsessively, hoping for good news. You apply to jobs you're overqualified for and underqualified for, just hoping someone will give you a chance.

This emotional state makes you vulnerable to manipulation. Scammers understand that unemployed people are dealing with damaged self-esteem and financial panic. They craft their schemes to offer exactly what you need most: immediate employment, good pay, and validation that you're valuable.

That fake job email plays into all of these needs. Work from home means no commute costs or professional wardrobe expenses. Flexible schedule suggests understanding employers who care about work-life balance. Higher-than-expected pay implies that someone finally recognizes your worth.

None of it was real, but it felt real because it addressed legitimate concerns about finding work that fits your situation.

The Evolution of Employment Scams

Twenty years ago, job scams were obvious. They involved stuffing envelopes at home or sending money to start your own business. The grammar was terrible, the promises were outrageous, and anyone with common sense could spot them.

Modern job scams are different. They use professional language, realistic job descriptions, and legitimate company names. They're posted on real job boards alongside genuine opportunities. They exploit current trends like remote work and gig economy jobs to seem relevant and attractive.

The scammers have also gotten better at psychological manipulation. Instead of promising thousands of dollars for no work, they offer slightly above-market rates for reasonable-sounding jobs. Instead of asking for large upfront payments, they request small fees for background checks or training materials.

These smaller requests feel more legitimate and are easier for desperate people to justify. "It's only $50 for a background check, and I'll make that back in the first few hours of work." Of course, there is no work, and the $50 is just the beginning.

The Pyramid Scheme Problem

You've been out of work for six months when you see a posting for "Marketing Associate" on a legitimate job board. The description mentions "building client relationships" and "promotional activities" with "unlimited earning potential based on performance."

The interview is at a nice office building, and the interviewer wears a suit. He talks about team building and personal development. He mentions that successful associates can earn six figures. He says the company is expanding rapidly and looking for motivated people to grow with them.

It all sounds professional until he explains that you'd be selling knives door-to-door and recruiting other people to do the same. Your income would come from sales commissions and a percentage of what the people you recruit sell. You'd have to buy a starter kit of sample knives for $200.

This isn't a marketing job. It's a multi-level marketing scheme, essentially a legal pyramid scheme. You'd make most of your money by recruiting other people to sell knives, who would recruit more people, and so on. The vast majority of people in these schemes lose money, but they're marketed as legitimate employment opportunities.

MLM companies target unemployed people because they're more likely to take risks and less likely to have other income sources. They use professional language and business settings to seem legitimate, but the business model is designed to benefit the people at the top while the people at the bottom lose money.

The Check Scam That Almost Worked

You think you've finally caught a break when a company offers you a remote bookkeeping job paying $25 an hour. After a brief phone interview, they say you're hired and will receive your first week's pay plus money to buy a computer and software for the job.

The check arrives by FedEx, which seems professional. It's for $2,847: $750 for your first week's pay and $2,097 for equipment. Your instructions are to deposit the check, keep your salary, and wire the equipment money to their "approved vendor" who will ship you everything you need.

You're suspicious enough to call your bank before doing anything. The customer service representative explains that this is a common scam. The check is fake, but banks are required to make funds available before they finish verifying checks. You would have wired real money from your account while thinking you were using the scammer's money. When the fake check bounces a few days later, you're responsible for the full amount.

The scammers were counting on you being unemployed and eager to start immediately. They created urgency by saying the equipment order needed to be placed right away so you could start training on Monday. They made it seem like you were helping your new employer by handling this transaction, when you were being set up to launder money.

Why Smart People Fall for Dumb Scams

You might think that only naive or desperate people fall for employment scams, but that's not true. Engineers, teachers, managers, and other educated professionals get taken by schemes that seem obvious in hindsight.

Unemployment does things to your brain. The constant rejection and financial stress affect your decision-making ability. You're more likely to see what you want to see and ignore warning signs that would normally make you suspicious.

The scammers also exploit this by making their victims feel special and chosen. "We've reviewed hundreds of resumes and yours stood out." "You have exactly the skills we're looking for." "We're only offering this opportunity to a select few people."

When you've been rejected by dozens of employers, hearing that someone wants you is intoxicating. It's hard to think clearly when someone is telling you that you're valuable and offering you exactly what you need.

Red Flags That Are Always Scams

These patterns appear in nearly every employment scam. If you see any of them, stop.

Real employers have hiring processes. They don't offer jobs without interviews, and they don't hire people based solely on resume reviews. If someone wants to employ you immediately without meeting you or talking to your references, something is wrong.

Real companies have real addresses and phone numbers. If you can't find a physical location for the business, or if their address turns out to be a strip mall or residential area, be suspicious. Legitimate businesses want customers and employees to be able to find them.

Real employers never ask you to pay them money. They don't charge for background checks, training materials, equipment, or processing fees. Any request for money, no matter how small or reasonable-sounding, is a scam.

Real job descriptions are detailed about duties, qualifications, and expectations. Fake postings use vague language about "earning money from home" or "being your own boss" because they don't have jobs to describe.

Real companies communicate professionally using company email addresses and proper grammar. If someone contacts you from a Gmail account with spelling errors and poor English, they're not representing a legitimate business.

What Happens When You Get Scammed

Getting scammed when you're unemployed isn't just about losing money. It's about having your hope manipulated when you're already vulnerable. It's about discovering that someone took advantage of your desperation to commit fraud.

The financial impact can be devastating when you're already struggling. If you send money for fake employment fees or fall for a check scam, you might lose money you can't afford to lose. If you give out personal information, you might become a victim of identity theft that takes months or years to resolve.

The emotional impact is often worse. You feel stupid for falling for something that seems obvious after the fact. You feel embarrassed about being taken advantage of. You might become paranoid about other opportunities, wondering if they're legitimate or just more elaborate scams.

This paranoia can hurt your job search by making you overly suspicious of real opportunities. Some legitimate employers use recruiters who contact people through LinkedIn. Some real companies do hire people quickly when they need to fill positions urgently. Some jobs do offer good pay for reasonable work.

How to Protect Yourself Without Becoming Paranoid

The goal isn't to assume that every opportunity is a scam. The goal is to verify that opportunities are legitimate before you invest time, money, or personal information in them.

Research every company that contacts you. Look them up online beyond their own website. Check for news articles, Better Business Bureau ratings, and employee reviews on sites like Glassdoor. Call their main number and ask about the position and the person who contacted you.

Be careful with personal information. Legitimate employers ask for your Social Security number and bank account information after they hire you, not during the application process. Don't give out sensitive information until you've verified that the company is real and the job offer is genuine.

Trust your instincts, but verify them with research. If something feels wrong, investigate further before proceeding. If something seems too good to be true, make sure it's true before you get excited about it.

Use your network to verify opportunities. Ask people in your industry if they've heard of the company or if the opportunity sounds legitimate. Other job seekers, former colleagues, and professional contacts can provide perspective when your judgment is clouded by desperation.

Moving Forward

One practical upside: learning to spot employment scams makes you better at evaluating all opportunities. The research habits you build — verifying companies, checking addresses, reading descriptions skeptically — protect you from legitimate but problematic employers who overpromise and underdeliver. Share what you know with other people in your network. The more people who recognize these patterns, the less effective the scams become.

Job search scams exist because unemployment creates vulnerability, and some people are willing to exploit that vulnerability for profit. You can't eliminate the risk entirely, but you can protect yourself by staying informed and thinking critically about opportunities.

Finding legitimate work takes time and effort. Anyone promising quick, easy money is lying to you. Focus on genuine opportunities with real companies that have real jobs. They exist, even if they're harder to find than the fake ones.

Don't let fear of scams make you miss real opportunities, but don't let desperation make you ignore obvious warning signs either. Trust the process, verify everything, and protect yourself. You'll find legitimate work eventually, and you'll do it without getting scammed in the process.

The unemployment experience is hard enough without having to worry about people trying to take advantage of you. Now you know what to watch for, and that knowledge will protect you throughout your career, not just during your job search.

Remote and Hybrid Work

The pandemic changed everything about where and how we work. What started as a temporary emergency measure became a permanent shift for millions of workers. Remote work went from a rare perk to a standard expectation in many industries.

If you're job searching now, you're navigating a work landscape that's fundamentally different from what existed five years ago. Some companies embraced remote work and never looked back. Others are desperately trying to get everyone back in the office. Most are somewhere in between, figuring out hybrid arrangements that nobody quite understands yet.

This creates opportunities and challenges you need to understand if you want to find work that fits your life and career goals.

The New Reality of Remote Work

Remote work isn't just about working from home anymore. It's become a defining feature of many job markets and a major factor in how people choose employers. The companies that figured out remote work early often have competitive advantages in hiring. The ones that didn't are struggling to attract talent.

Remote work isn't available everywhere or for everyone. Manufacturing, healthcare, retail, and service industries still require physical presence. Even within office-based industries, some roles translate well to remote work while others don't.

Understanding which jobs and companies offer meaningful remote work helps you focus your search effectively. A lot of job postings mention "remote work" but mean something different than what you might expect.

"Fully remote" means you can work from anywhere, possibly with occasional travel to company offices. "Remote-first" means the company is designed around remote work, with systems and culture built for distributed teams. "Remote-friendly" often means they allow some remote work but still expect regular office presence.

"Hybrid" arrangements vary wildly. Some companies want you in the office three days a week. Others expect monthly visits. Some let teams decide their own schedules. The term "hybrid" has become meaningless without details about expectations.

"Temporary remote" describes companies that went remote during COVID but plan to return to full-time office work. These arrangements are unstable and not good bets if you need long-term remote work.

Finding Legitimate Remote Opportunities

The explosion of remote work also created an explosion of remote work scams. Fake job postings promising easy money for "remote data entry" or "online customer service" have proliferated alongside legitimate opportunities.

Real remote jobs are posted on mainstream job boards like Indeed, LinkedIn, and company websites. They have job descriptions, realistic salary ranges, and identifiable companies with real addresses and phone numbers. The hiring process includes video interviews with hiring managers, not just email exchanges with "HR departments."

Remote job boards like FlexJobs, Remote.co, and We Work Remotely focus on legitimate remote opportunities. These sites screen postings and charge employers to list positions, reducing the likelihood of scams.

Look for remote jobs at companies that were already distributed before COVID. These organizations have mature remote work practices and are less likely to suddenly change their policies. Companies like GitLab, Buffer, Zapier, and Automattic built their entire operations around remote work.

Tech companies, digital marketing agencies, accounting firms, and consulting organizations often have well-developed remote work programs. Media companies, educational institutions, and nonprofits also frequently offer remote positions.

Avoid "remote" jobs that require you to live in a city or region unless that makes sense for the role. If a company claims to offer remote work but insists you live within commuting distance of their office, they haven't committed to real remote work.

Presenting Yourself as a Remote Candidate

Employers have legitimate concerns about remote workers. They worry about productivity, communication, and culture fit. Your job application and interview process need to address these concerns proactively.

Highlight any previous remote work experience, even if it was part-time or temporary. COVID-forced remote work counts. Freelance projects, consulting work, and volunteer activities that required remote collaboration all demonstrate your ability to work independently.

If you don't have remote work experience, emphasize skills that translate well: self-motivation, strong written communication, time management, and familiarity with digital collaboration tools. Mention software you've used: Slack, Zoom, Microsoft Teams, Google Workspace, project management tools.

Your home office setup matters more than you might think. You don't need an expensive setup, but you need a quiet space for video calls, reliable internet, and basic equipment that works consistently. Be prepared to describe your workspace during interviews.

Communication skills become more important in remote work. Everything that would normally happen through casual office interactions needs to be intentional and digital. Strong writing skills, comfort with video calls, and ability to ask questions clearly become essential job qualifications.

Time zone considerations affect many remote positions. If a company operates primarily in Eastern time but you live on the

West Coast, understand how that affects meeting schedules and collaboration expectations. Some companies are flexible about time zones; others expect hours regardless of your location.

The Remote Interview Process

Video interviews are now standard for remote positions, and how you handle the technical and interpersonal aspects sends signals about your remote work readiness.

Test your technology before every interview. Check your internet connection, camera, microphone, and lighting. Have backup plans for technical failures: a phone number to call, alternative internet access, a different device if your main computer fails.

Your video setup should be professional but not elaborate. Good lighting (facing a window works well), a clean background, and a stable camera angle matter more than expensive equipment. Avoid virtual backgrounds unless you're confident they work smoothly with your setup.

Dress professionally for video interviews, at least from the waist up. Treat the interview with the same formality you'd use for an in-person meeting. You're demonstrating that you can maintain professional standards while working from home.

Practice making eye contact with the camera instead of looking at the screen. This creates the impression of direct eye contact with the interviewer. It feels unnatural at first but makes a difference in how you're perceived.

Be prepared for questions about your remote work preferences and capabilities. "How do you stay motivated when working alone?" "How do you handle communication with team members in different time zones?" "What's your experience with remote collaboration tools?" These questions assess your thoughtfulness about remote work challenges.

Skills and Setup for Remote Success

Remote work requires some technical competencies that might not be necessary for office-based roles. Employers expect remote workers to be reasonably self-sufficient with technology and digital communication.

Basic video conferencing skills are essential. You should be comfortable with Zoom, Microsoft Teams, Google Meet, and similar platforms. Know how to screen share, use chat functions, mute and unmute yourself appropriately, and troubleshoot basic technical issues.

Familiarity with cloud-based collaboration tools is increasingly important. Google Workspace, Microsoft 365, Slack, Asana, Trello, and similar platforms enable remote teamwork. You don't need to be an expert in all of them, but comfort with digital collaboration concepts helps.

Project management and organization skills become more visible in remote work. When you're not physically present, your work product and communication become the primary ways colleagues assess your performance. Strong organizational systems help you deliver consistent results.

Written communication skills matter more in remote work because so much communication happens through email, chat, and document collaboration. Clear, concise writing helps prevent misunderstandings that are easier to resolve quickly in person.

Your home office doesn't need to be elaborate, but it should support productive work. A dedicated workspace, even if it's just a corner of a room, helps create boundaries between work and personal life. Reliable internet, a comfortable chair, and good lighting are more important than expensive furniture.

Compensation Considerations

Remote work affects salary negotiations in complex ways. Some companies pay the same regardless of location. Others adjust salaries based on local cost of living. Still others offer location-independent salaries but set them based on their headquarters location.

Geographic pay differences can be significant. A company based in San Francisco might pay San Francisco salaries to all remote workers, benefiting people living in lower-cost areas. Conversely, a company might adjust salaries downward for remote workers in less expensive locations.

Understand a company's remote pay policy before negotiating salary. If they adjust for location, factor that into your compensation expectations and cost-of-living calculations. A lower salary might still result in higher take-home pay if you live in an area with lower housing costs.

Consider the total value of remote work when evaluating offers. No commute saves money on gas, parking, car maintenance, and work clothes. Eating lunch at home is cheaper than buying meals near the office. These savings can offset lower salaries for remote positions.

Some remote workers face additional costs: higher utility bills, home office equipment, and upgraded internet service. Factor these expenses into your budget when considering remote opportunities.

Building Relationships and Visibility

One of the biggest challenges in remote work is building relationships and maintaining visibility with colleagues and supervisors. Out of sight can become out of mind when promotion and project opportunities arise.

Proactive communication becomes essential in remote work. Regular check-ins with supervisors, active participation in team meetings, and voluntary updates about project progress help maintain your presence in colleagues' awareness.

Video calls create more personal connections than phone calls or email. Turn on your camera for meetings when possible, and suggest video calls for one-on-one conversations. Seeing faces helps build relationships that pure audio or text communication can't replicate.

Informal relationship building requires more intention in remote work. The casual conversations that happen naturally in office environments need to be created deliberately through virtual coffee chats, online team activities, or informal video calls.

Document your work and contributions more thoroughly than you might in an office environment. When your work isn't visible through physical presence, written records of your accomplishments become more important for performance reviews and career advancement.

Participate actively in company culture initiatives, even virtual ones. Online team building, digital social events, and company-wide communications help you stay connected to organizational culture and relationships.

Managing Work-Life Balance Remotely

Working from home can blur boundaries between work and personal life in ways that create both opportunities and challenges. Without physical separation between office and home, maintaining balance requires deliberate strategies.

Create physical and temporal boundaries between work and personal time. A dedicated workspace helps, even if it's just a chair or corner of a room. Set work hours and stick to them, especially when colleagues are in different time zones and might expect responses at unusual hours.

The flexibility of remote work can be both a benefit and a trap. You might have more flexibility to handle personal responsibilities during work hours, but that can lead to working longer total hours to compensate. Track your work time to ensure you're not consistently working more than you're paid for.

Isolation is a real challenge for some remote workers. The social interaction that happens naturally in offices needs to be replaced with intentional social connections. Some people thrive with less social interaction; others find remote work lonely and demotivating.

Home distractions affect some people more than others. Family members, household chores, personal errands, and entertainment options compete for attention in ways that don't exist in office environments. Successful remote workers develop strategies for managing these distractions.

Career Advancement in Remote Work

Career development works differently in remote environments. The informal mentoring, networking, and visibility that drive advancement in traditional offices need to be recreated intentionally in remote settings.

Seek out mentoring relationships more proactively in remote work. Without casual office interactions, mentoring needs to be more structured and intentional. Request regular one-on-one meetings with supervisors and senior colleagues who can provide career guidance.

Professional development opportunities might be more accessible in remote work environments. Online conferences, webinars, and training programs eliminate travel requirements and might be more available to remote workers than in-person alternatives.

Networking requires different strategies for remote workers. Industry associations, online professional communities, and virtual events replace in-person networking opportunities. Building professional relationships online takes different skills than traditional face-to-face networking.

Document your contributions and achievements more systematically in remote work. Without daily visibility, your accomplishments need to be communicated more explicitly through performance reviews, project summaries, and regular updates to supervisors.

The Return-to-Office Tension

Many companies are still figuring out their long-term remote work policies. Some that embraced remote work during COVID are now requiring return to office. Others are moving in the opposite direction, becoming fully remote to access broader talent pools.

This uncertainty creates risks for job seekers who need remote work. A company that currently offers remote work might change its policies after you're hired. Understanding a company's commitment to remote work helps assess the stability of remote arrangements.

Look for signals about a company's remote work commitment. Companies that invested in remote work infrastructure, hired employees far from their offices, and incorporated remote work into their public messaging are less likely to suddenly require return to office.

Be wary of companies that seem ambivalent about remote work or describe it as a temporary accommodation. If remote work is important to you, target companies that view it as a permanent competitive advantage instead of a necessary evil.

Some companies are developing hybrid policies that require office days or regular in-person presence. Understand these requirements clearly before accepting offers. "Hybrid" can mean anything from one day per month to four days per week in the office.

Industry and Role Considerations

Remote work availability varies significantly across industries and job functions. Understanding these patterns helps focus your search on realistic opportunities.

Technology, marketing, finance, writing, design, and consulting translate well to remote work. These fields involve primarily knowledge work that can be done from anywhere with good internet access.

Sales roles are increasingly remote-friendly, especially when they involve phone or video client interactions instead of in-person meetings. Customer service and support roles often work well remotely, though some companies prefer call center environments.

Management and leadership roles present mixed opportunities for remote work. Some companies embrace remote leadership; others believe management requires physical presence. This varies by company culture and industry.

Creative roles like graphic design, writing, and video production often work well remotely. Collaborative creative work sometimes suffers without in-person brainstorming and feedback sessions.

Education has embraced remote work more since COVID, with opportunities in online teaching, instructional design, and educational technology. Healthcare has limited remote opportunities, mostly in telehealth, medical coding, and administrative functions.

Making Remote Work Sustainable

Remote work isn't automatically better than office work. It suits some personality types, work styles, and life situations better than others. Honest self-assessment helps determine whether remote work aligns with your preferences and capabilities.

Consider your communication style and preferences. People who thrive on frequent face-to-face interaction might struggle with remote work. Those who prefer written communication and independent work often love remote arrangements.

Evaluate your home environment realistically. Shared living spaces, unreliable internet, or frequent interruptions can make remote work challenging. You don't need a perfect setup, but you need conditions that support productive work.

Think about your career goals and how remote work affects them. Some career paths benefit from the networking and mentoring opportunities that in-person work provides. Others advance just as well or better in remote environments.

Remote work requires self-motivation and time management skills that some people need to develop. If you thrive with external structure and supervision, remote work might require adjusting your work habits and accountability systems.

Moving Forward with Remote Work

Remote work is now a permanent part of the employment landscape, but it's not universally available or universally beneficial. Understanding how it fits your career goals, work style, and life situation helps you make informed decisions about pursuing remote opportunities.

The companies that have embraced remote work as a competitive advantage are often better employers overall. They tend to focus on results instead of hours, trust employees to manage their work, and offer the flexibility that many people need for work-life balance.

Don't assume that all remote work opportunities are equal. The quality of remote work experiences varies dramatically based on company culture, management practices, and team dynamics. A bad remote job can be worse than a mediocre office job.

Use remote work as one factor among many in your job search. It's an important consideration, but it shouldn't override other factors like career development opportunities, compensation, company culture, and alignment with your professional goals.

The future likely includes more remote and hybrid work options, but the arrangements will continue evolving. Stay flexible about work arrangements while being clear about your own preferences and requirements.

Remote work represents a fundamental shift in how we think about employment, location, and work-life integration. Whether it's right for you depends on your circumstances, but understanding how to navigate this new landscape is essential for modern job searching.

When Your Situation Is Complicated

Most unemployment situations follow predictable patterns, but some circumstances require different strategies. Maybe you were fired instead of laid off. Maybe your entire industry is collapsing. Maybe the economy tanked and everyone is competing for the same few jobs. Here's how to handle the complications that don't fit the standard playbook.

When You Get Fired vs. Laid Off

Getting fired and getting laid off are legally and practically different, even though they both leave you unemployed. Understanding the difference affects how you explain your situation to potential employers and what benefits you might be entitled to.

Getting laid off means your position was eliminated for business reasons: budget cuts, restructuring, company closure, or economic conditions. It's not about your performance. You're usually eligible for unemployment benefits and might get severance pay.

Getting fired means you were terminated for cause: poor performance, violating company policy, or other conduct issues. You might not be eligible for unemployment benefits, and you definitely won't get severance.

If you were laid off, this is easier to explain to employers because it wasn't about you personally. "The company eliminated my position due to budget constraints" or "They closed the entire department" are straightforward explanations that don't raise red flags.

If you were fired, this is trickier. You need to be honest without destroying your chances. Practice a brief, factual explanation that takes responsibility without going into detail: "It wasn't a good fit" or "I learned valuable lessons about what I need in a work environment."

Don't bash your former employer, even if they treated you badly. Don't lie about being fired because employers can verify this information. Focus on what you learned and how you've grown since then.

Sometimes the distinction isn't clear. You might have been "laid off" but everyone knows it was really because your boss didn't like you. Or you might have been fired, but the real reason was that the company was cutting costs and used your performance as an excuse.

In these gray situations, use your judgment about how to present it. The goal is honesty without self-sabotage.

Unemployment During Economic Downturns

When the entire economy tanks, unemployment becomes a different game. Instead of competing with a few other candidates, you're competing with hundreds. Companies stop hiring, hiring managers become picky, and the process takes longer.

During recessions, more people compete for fewer jobs. Employers can be extremely selective. Salary offers are lower. Hiring processes take longer. Companies prioritize "safe" candidates with perfect qualifications. Networking becomes even more important because so many people are applying for posted jobs.

You need different strategies for recession job searching. Lower your salary expectations temporarily. Consider jobs slightly below your previous level. Be open to contract or temporary work. Focus heavily on networking since posted jobs get flooded with applications. Target essential industries that are still hiring: healthcare, utilities, government. Be prepared for longer job searches.

Don't make these recession mistakes. Don't wait for the economy to improve before looking seriously. Don't be too picky about jobs when you need income. Don't assume you can wait out the recession on savings. Don't ignore industries you hadn't considered before.

The upside? Everyone understands that unemployment during a recession isn't about you personally. Employers are more sympathetic to employment gaps during obvious economic downturns.

The Reference Problem

References can make or break your job search, but what do you do when your references are problematic? Maybe your former boss hates you. Maybe your company went out of business and everyone scattered. Maybe you've been out of work so long that your references are stale.

When your former boss will give you a bad reference, first find out what they're saying. Have a friend call pretending to be checking references, or use a professional reference checking service. You need to know what you're dealing with.

If it's bad, try to use other people from the same company: colleagues, clients, people from other departments who knew your work. HR departments often have policies about only confirming dates of employment and salary, which might be better than a personal opinion from your boss.

Consider addressing it proactively with potential employers: "My relationship with my former manager wasn't great, but I can provide references from colleagues who worked closely with me."

When your company went out of business, this is easier to handle than you might think. Use former colleagues who have moved to other companies. Use clients or vendors who worked with you. Explain the situation to potential employers. They understand that business closures scatter former coworkers.

If you've been out of work for a long time, your professional references might not remember you well or might not be current with your recent efforts to stay engaged. Supplement old professional references with newer ones from volunteer work, professional development courses, or freelance projects. A reference from a nonprofit where you've been volunteering recently might be more valuable than a lukewarm reference from a job you left three years ago.

You can build new references by volunteering in your field or related areas. Take classes and build relationships with instructors. Do freelance or consulting work. Join professional associations and get involved. Attend industry events and maintain relationships.

Some employers are moving away from traditional references because they're time-consuming and often not helpful. Be prepared for background checks, skills assessments, or portfolio reviews instead.

When Your Industry Is Dying

Some unemployment happens because entire industries become obsolete. Technology changes, consumer preferences shift, or economic forces make entire categories of work disappear.

If you're a coal miner, newspaper reporter, travel agent, or in another declining industry, you can't just wait for things to improve. You need to figure out how to transfer your skills to growing fields.

Traditional retail is being replaced by e-commerce. Print media is shrinking as newspapers and magazines close. Coal mining and some other extraction industries are declining. Traditional banking is being automated. Some manufacturing has moved overseas or been automated. Traditional taxi services have been replaced by rideshare apps.

Accept reality first. Your industry might recover partially, but it's not going back to what it was. You need to adapt.

Then identify transferable skills. What did you do in your old job that applies to other industries? Customer service, project management, problem-solving, team leadership, and technical skills often transfer.

Research growing industries that need your skills. Healthcare, technology, renewable energy, and logistics are growing. Where do your skills fit?

Get additional training if needed. Community colleges, online courses, and professional certifications can help you bridge from your old industry to a new one.

Network in your new target industry. Your old industry contacts won't help much if that industry is disappearing.

Some transitions work well. Newspaper reporters become corporate communications specialists or content marketers. Coal miners become solar panel installers or wind turbine technicians. Travel agents become event planners or corporate travel coordinators. Bank tellers become customer service representatives or office administrators.

Leaving a dying industry feels like admitting defeat, especially if you spent decades building expertise. But staying in a shrinking field is usually worse than starting over in a growing one.

Legal Issues and Wrongful Termination

Most employment is "at will," meaning you can be fired for any reason or no reason, as long as it's not illegal discrimination. But sometimes firings are illegal, and you might have legal recourse.

Termination might be illegal if it's discrimination based on race, gender, age, religion, disability, or other protected characteristics. Retaliation for filing complaints about illegal activity or harassment is also illegal. Violations of employment contracts or company policies can be grounds for legal action. Being fired for refusing to do something illegal is also protected.

If you think you were wrongfully terminated, consult an employment lawyer for a free consultation. Most work on contingency, so they only get paid if you win. Document everything you remember about the circumstances of your firing.

Don't let legal issues derail your job search. Even if you have a legitimate legal claim, pursue it separately from finding new work. Lawsuits take years, and you need income now.

Be careful about discussing legal issues with potential employers. You don't want to seem like someone who sues former employers, even if your case is legitimate.

Non-Compete Clauses and Legal Restrictions

Some employment agreements include non-compete clauses that legally restrict where you can work after leaving. These vary widely by state and industry.

Read your employment agreement carefully. Non-compete clauses typically restrict you from working for competitors or starting competing businesses for a set time period in a certain geographic area.

Enforceability varies by state. Some states like California don't enforce non-compete agreements at all. Others enforce them strictly. If you're unsure, consult an employment lawyer.

You might be able to work in the same industry for non-competing companies, or in different industries using your skills differently. Focus on opportunities that clearly don't violate your agreement.

If your non-compete agreement makes it impossible to work in your field, you might be able to challenge it legally. Courts sometimes refuse to enforce agreements that are too broad or prevent someone from earning a living.

When You've Been Out of Work for Years

Long-term unemployment creates special challenges. The longer you're out of work, the harder it becomes to get back in.

Employers worry about why you've been unemployed so long and whether your skills are current.

Be honest but strategic about how you explain long gaps. Health issues, family caregiving, and education are generally acceptable explanations. "I took time to reassess my career goals" works for shorter gaps but becomes less believable after a year.

Stay current during long unemployment by taking online courses in your field. Volunteer in professional roles. Do freelance or consulting work. Attend industry events and maintain professional relationships. Keep up with industry news and trends.

Consider temporary, part-time, or contract work to get back into professional environments. These can lead to permanent opportunities and help you rebuild confidence and references.

Don't apologize for unemployment. Present your time out of work as a deliberate choice when possible, not as a series of rejections. "I took time to care for my elderly mother" or "I used the time to update my skills" sounds better than "I couldn't find anything."

Working with Recruiters and Staffing Agencies

External recruiters and staffing agencies can be helpful, but they work for employers, not for you. Understanding their motivations helps you work with them effectively.

Retained recruiters are paid by companies to find candidates for senior positions. Contingency recruiters only get paid if they place someone. Staffing agencies place people in temporary or contract positions.

Be honest about your situation and requirements when working with recruiters. Respond promptly to their communications. Don't work with too many recruiters on the same search. Understand that they have multiple candidates for each position.

Watch out for red flags. Recruiters who ask you to pay fees are scams. Be wary of those who are vague about which company or position they're recruiting for. Don't work with recruiters who pressure you to accept offers without giving you time to consider them, or who aren't transparent about salary ranges or job requirements.

When Unemployment Benefits Are Denied

Not everyone who loses their job qualifies for unemployment benefits. If your claim is denied, you might still have options.

Claims get denied when you were fired for misconduct, quit voluntarily, haven't worked long enough or earned enough to qualify, or aren't actively looking for work.

You can appeal unemployment benefit denials, and many appeals are successful. The process varies by state, but you typically get a hearing where you can present your case.

Legal aid organizations sometimes help with unemployment appeals. Some areas have advocacy groups that focus on unemployment issues.

Continue looking for work and document your job search activities, even while appealing a benefits denial. You might still qualify for benefits for part of your unemployment period.

Moving Forward with Special Circumstances

Whatever circumstances you're facing, the key is adapting your strategy while maintaining momentum in your job search. Don't let unique challenges become excuses for not looking for work.

Most employers understand that career paths aren't always smooth. Economic downturns, industry changes, and personal circumstances create complications that aren't your fault. Focus on what you can control: your skills, your presentation, and your effort.

The job market has room for people with complicated backgrounds and non-linear career paths. You just need to be strategic about how you present your situation and persistent about finding opportunities that fit your circumstances.

Your complications might become advantages with the right employers. Someone who has navigated industry changes, legal challenges, or long unemployment periods might have resilience and problem-solving skills that other candidates lack.

Don't let perfect be the enemy of good. The goal isn't to find an employer who doesn't care about your complications. The goal is to find one who values what you bring despite those complications.

When You're Young and Already Screwed

If you're under 30 and unemployed, everyone has an opinion about your situation. Older people think you're entitled and don't want to work hard. Your parents think you're not trying hard enough. Your friends with jobs think you're unlucky. Career advisors tell you this is "normal" for your generation.

They're all wrong.

Being young and unemployed isn't the same as being older and unemployed. You face different challenges, different judgments, and different pressures. The advice that works for someone with 20 years of experience doesn't work for someone trying to get their first real job.

Here's what you need to know about navigating unemployment when you're young, broke, and tired of living in your childhood bedroom.

The Unique Hell of Young Unemployment

When you're young and unemployed, everyone assumes it's your fault. You must be picky, lazy, or unrealistic about what jobs you're willing to take. You must be living off your parents and not feeling urgency to find work.

The reality is different. You're competing with people who have more experience for every entry-level job. You're told you need experience to get experience. You're offered unpaid internships when you need to pay rent. You're asked to have skills nobody taught you and knowledge about industries you've never worked in.

Meanwhile, you're watching friends get jobs, start careers, move out of their parents' houses, and begin adult lives while you're stuck in limbo. The pressure to figure out your entire career path while unemployed is overwhelming.

The Experience Paradox

Every job posting says "entry-level" but requires 2-3 years of experience. This isn't a mistake or oversight. It's how the job market works now, and it's broken in ways that hurt young people most.

Companies post entry-level jobs requiring experience because they can. There are enough desperate candidates that someone will apply who has the experience, even if they're overqualified. The "entry-level" label is there to justify paying less money.

You have several options for dealing with this: lie about your experience (not recommended), find ways to get experience outside traditional jobs, focus on companies that hire new graduates, or consider jobs that don't require experience even if they're not perfect matches.

The goal isn't to find the perfect entry-level job. The goal is to get any job that gives you professional experience and a paycheck. Your first job doesn't define your career.

The Gig Economy Trap

You've been told that freelancing, gig work, and the "hustle economy" are great opportunities for young people. Sometimes that's true. Usually, it's a way to exploit your desperation.

Gig work can be useful for immediate income while job searching, but don't mistake it for career building. Driving for rideshare companies or delivering food might pay bills, but it doesn't give you professional experience or advancement opportunities.

Be wary of "marketing" jobs that turn out to be door-to-door sales, "management training" programs that are pyramid schemes, and "entrepreneurship opportunities" that require you to pay money upfront.

If something sounds too good to be true (work from home! Set your own hours! Unlimited earning potential!), it probably is.

Legitimate entry-level jobs exist, but they're not usually advertised with exclamation points.

Living with Your Parents (Again)

Moving back in with your parents after college feels like failure, but it's become normal for young adults. More than half of people under 25 live with family members, often because of financial necessity instead of choice.

This living situation affects your job search in ways you might not expect. Some employers judge candidates who live with parents, assuming they're not serious about work or independence. Some geographic limitations make it harder to find jobs or attend interviews.

Living with family can give you financial flexibility to be more selective about jobs and take unpaid internships that lead to better opportunities. Use this advantage strategically instead of feeling ashamed about it.

Set boundaries with family about your job search. Parents who supported you through college might have opinions about what jobs you should take or how you should search. Listen to advice, but make your own decisions.

The Student Loan Reality

You're dealing with student loan debt while unemployed, adding financial pressure and limiting your options. Forbearance and deferment can provide temporary relief, but interest keeps accumulating.

Don't ignore your loans hoping they'll go away. Contact your loan servicer to discuss options like income-driven repayment plans or temporary hardship deferrals. The worst thing you can do is default.

Factor loan payments into your job search decisions. A lower-paying job that allows you to make minimum payments might be better than holding out for a higher salary while accumulating interest and late fees.

Consider jobs with loan forgiveness programs in public service, education, or healthcare. These programs have strict requirements, but they can eliminate debt if you qualify.

Networking When You Have No Network

Everyone tells you to network, but networking is harder when you're young because you don't have professional relationships yet. Your network consists of classmates, professors, family friends, and people from part-time jobs.

Start with what you have. Professors often have industry connections and want to help former students. Family friends might know about opportunities in their companies. Alumni networks from your school can be valuable for making connections.

Don't dismiss connections from part-time jobs, internships, or volunteer work. The manager from your retail job might have moved to a different company. The supervisor from your internship might know about openings in other departments.

Use social media strategically. LinkedIn is obvious, but Twitter and Instagram can also help you connect with people in industries you're interested in. Follow companies and industry leaders, engage with their content, and participate in professional discussions.

The Overqualification Problem

If you have a college degree, you might be told you're overqualified for jobs that don't require degrees. This is frustrating when you need income and experience, but employers worry that you'll leave as soon as something better comes along.

Address this concern directly in cover letters and interviews. Explain why you're interested in the role and the company. Show enthusiasm for the work itself, not just the paycheck.

Be honest about your career goals without making employers feel like you're using them as a stepping stone. It's okay to say you're interested in learning about the industry or developing skills.

Consider removing your degree from applications for jobs where it's not required, in retail, food service, or customer service. This might feel like you're hiding an accomplishment, but it can help you get interviews.

Entry-Level Job Search Strategy

Apply broadly but strategically. Don't just apply to jobs with "entry-level" in the title. Look for roles asking for 0-2 years of experience, coordinator positions, assistant roles, and trainee programs.

Target companies known for hiring new graduates. Large corporations often have formal training programs for recent graduates. Small companies might be more willing to train someone without experience.

Apply to jobs even if you don't meet every requirement. Job postings are wish lists, not strict requirements. If you meet 60-70% of the qualifications, apply anyway.

Customize your applications for each job, but don't spend hours perfecting each one. Volume matters when you're competing with many other candidates. Aim for good enough instead of perfect.

Interview Strategies for New Graduates

Employers expect you to lack experience, so focus on potential instead of past accomplishments. Talk about what you've learned in school, internships, volunteer work, or personal projects.

Prepare examples that demonstrate soft skills: teamwork, problem-solving, communication, adaptability. These matter more than technical skills for most entry-level positions.

Show enthusiasm and willingness to learn. Employers hire new graduates expecting to train them. Your attitude matters more than your knowledge.

Ask thoughtful questions about training, mentorship, and growth opportunities. This shows you're thinking long-term and interested in developing your career.

The Side Hustle Reality

Side hustles can supplement income while job searching, but be realistic about their potential. Most successful side hustles take months or years to generate income.

Focus on side work that builds relevant skills or makes professional connections. Freelance writing, social media management, or tutoring might lead to full-time opportunities.

Don't let side hustles replace job searching entirely. It's tempting to focus on entrepreneurial projects instead of applying for traditional jobs, but most side hustles don't provide stable income or benefits.

Dealing with Judgment and Pressure

Young unemployment comes with social stigma that older unemployed people don't face. You're judged for living with parents, not having a career plan, or taking jobs that aren't related to your degree.

Ignore most of this judgment. People who haven't job searched recently don't understand current market conditions. Your parents' generation could walk into companies and get hired on the spot. That world doesn't exist anymore.

Set realistic expectations for yourself and your family. Your first job won't be your dream job. Your career path won't be linear. That's normal for your generation.

Building Experience Without Traditional Jobs

If you can't find traditional employment, look for other ways to build relevant experience. Volunteer with organizations in your target industry. Take on freelance projects. Start a blog or portfolio showcasing your skills.

Consider certificate programs or online courses that demonstrate current skills. Many are free or low-cost and can make your resume more competitive.

Join professional associations as a student member. Attend events, participate in online discussions, and volunteer for committees. This provides networking opportunities and industry knowledge.

The Mental Health Challenge

Young unemployment can be damaging to mental health because it affects your sense of identity and future prospects during a crucial developmental period.

Don't underestimate the psychological impact of rejection, financial stress, and social pressure. If you're struggling with depression or anxiety, get professional help. Many colleges offer alumni counseling services.

Your career doesn't define your worth as a person. Unemployment is a temporary situation, not a reflection of your value or potential.

Long-Term Perspective

Your first job matters less than you think. Very few people stay in their first job for their entire career. The goal is getting professional experience and figuring out what you want to do next.

Your twenties are for experimenting, learning, and making mistakes. Don't put pressure on yourself to have everything figured out immediately.

The job market will change during your career. Skills that matter today might be obsolete in ten years. Focus on developing adaptability and learning ability instead of specific technical knowledge.

Practical Next Steps

Apply for unemployment benefits if you're eligible. Some states allow recent graduates to collect benefits even without extensive work history.

Take advantage of resources for young job seekers. Many cities have organizations focused on helping new graduates find work.

Consider temporary or contract work. These positions often lead to permanent opportunities and give you experience in different companies and industries.

Don't turn down jobs because they're not perfect. Your goal is getting experience and income, not finding your life's work in your first position.

The Truth About Your Generation

Despite what older people say, your generation isn't entitled or lazy. You're dealing with economic conditions that are more difficult than what previous generations faced. Student debt is higher, entry-level wages are lower (adjusted for inflation), and job security is nonexistent.

You're also more educated, more diverse, and more technologically capable than previous generations. These are advantages, even if they don't feel like it when you're unemployed.

Your career will likely be different from your parents' careers. You'll change jobs more frequently, work for different types of companies, and have more varied experiences. This isn't necessarily bad, it's just different.

Being young and unemployed is frustrating. It's also temporary. The job market is broken in specific, diagnosable ways — not in ways that have anything to do with your worth. Figure out which lever is broken. Fix it. Keep applying the Job Search Inversion. Most people who do the right things consistently get somewhere eventually.

The first job is just the first job. It doesn't define the rest.

Conclusion: You Made It Through

If you're reading this, you either found a job or you're still looking. Either way, you've survived unemployment longer than you thought you could when this all started.

That's not nothing. Unemployment tests every part of your life: your finances, your relationships, your mental health, your sense of self-worth. You're still here, still working the problem.

What You've Learned

Unemployment teaches you things you never wanted to learn. You've learned that job security is a myth. You've learned that the hiring process is broken and frustrating. You've learned that rejection doesn't mean you're not good enough.

You've learned to budget when money is tight. You've learned to network when you don't feel like it. You've learned to interview when your confidence is shot. You've learned to negotiate when you have no leverage.

You've learned that your career isn't your identity, even though it feels like it sometimes. You've learned that your worth as a person isn't determined by your employment status. You've learned that you can survive things you didn't think you could survive.

These are hard lessons, but they're valuable ones. You'll never take a job for granted again. You'll never assume that employment is permanent. You'll always have a backup plan because you've learned what happens when you don't have one.

If You Found a Job

You got a job. That's the thing that needed to happen and it happened. Now don't waste the first week of it coasting on relief.

Your new job isn't perfect. It might not pay what you want, or offer the title you hoped for, or be exactly what you imagined.

That's okay. Perfect jobs are rare, and first jobs after unemployment are often stepping stones to something better.

What matters is that you're employed again. You have income, structure, purpose, and professional identity. You can start rebuilding your financial security and planning for the future.

Don't forget what unemployment taught you. Stay connected to your network. Keep your resume updated. Save money for the next time something unexpected happens. Because there will be a next time, even if it's years away.

Build relationships at your new job, but don't become completely dependent on it for your security. The goal isn't just to have a job. The goal is to build a career that can survive the next layoff, merger, or economic downturn.

Use this experience to help other people. When you meet someone who's unemployed, don't give them generic advice about "staying positive." Give them practical help: introductions, job leads, honest feedback about their search strategy. You know what it's like to be where they are.

If You're Still Looking

You're not done yet, but you're not defeated either. Finding work takes time, and sometimes it takes longer than you expect or want. That doesn't mean you're doing anything wrong.

Each interview is practice. Each conversation builds a relationship that may matter later. The process is not random — it rewards consistency, specificity, and relationships over volume and luck.

Most people find work. If you haven't yet, something specific is broken. Use the Three-Lever Diagnosis: targeting, materials, or relationships. Figure out which one it is. Fix that one thing.

If you've been looking for a long time, it might be time to reconsider your strategy. Are you being too selective about opportunities? Are you presenting yourself effectively? Are you networking in the right places? Sometimes small changes in approach can make a big difference in results.

If it's taking longer than you expected, that's normal. If nothing is moving after 60 days, something is broken. The difference matters — one requires patience, the other requires a diagnosis.

What Happens Next

Your relationship with work will never be the same after unemployment. You'll always be a little more cautious, a little more prepared, a little less trusting of corporate promises about job security.

That's not pessimism, it's realism. The social contract between employers and employees has changed. Companies will eliminate positions whenever it serves their financial interests. Understanding this reality helps you make better decisions about your career.

You'll change jobs more frequently than previous generations did. You'll need to stay current with skills and maintain professional relationships outside your immediate workplace. You'll need to think strategically about your career instead of just showing up and hoping for the best.

This isn't necessarily bad. Having multiple experiences at different companies can make you more valuable and more adaptable. Building a diverse network can create more opportunities. Developing portable skills can protect you from industry changes.

The key is being intentional about your career instead of letting it happen to you. Unemployment forces you to think strategically about work, and that's a skill that will serve you well.

Final Thoughts

Unemployment is one of the most stressful experiences most people face. It attacks your identity, your finances, your relationships, and your sense of security all at once. Dealing with it doesn't make you weak or unsuccessful. It makes you human.

The advice in this book isn't magic. It won't guarantee that you'll find work immediately or that the process will be easy. What it will do is help you avoid common mistakes and focus your energy on the things that matter.

Job searching is a skill, and like any skill, you get better at it with practice. Unfortunately, most people only practice when they have to, when they're stressed and desperate. Do your best with the situation you're in, and remember that you're learning skills you'll hopefully never need again.

Take care of yourself during this process. Unemployment is a marathon, not a sprint. You need to pace yourself and maintain your physical and mental health. You can't perform well in interviews or network effectively if you're falling apart.

Most people find work within six months to a year. Some faster, some slower. The ones who take longer usually have a specific problem in their approach — wrong target, weak network, resume that isn't converting — not a fundamental flaw in who they are. Diagnose the problem. Fix it. Keep moving.

When you land something, don't let it happen to you the same way the last job did. You know things now you didn't know before: that job security is a management decision, not a loyalty reward. That your network is your actual safety net. That the gap between employed and unemployed is smaller and faster than it looks from inside a steady paycheck.

Use that knowledge. That's the only good thing unemployment reliably produces.

Now turn the page and start the checklist.

Good luck.

Your First Week: Damage Control

File for unemployment benefits. Don't wait. Get written confirmation of your termination date, final pay, and benefits status from HR. Find out when your health insurance ends and what your COBRA options are. Do not sign any severance agreement without reading it carefully — most give you 21 days to decide. Save any personal files from company systems before access is cut. Tell six people in your professional network that you're looking.

Your First Month: Get the Foundation Right

Write out your monthly budget and calculate exactly how long your money lasts. Rewrite your resume from scratch with specific accomplishments and numbers. Overhaul your LinkedIn profile. Define the specific type of role and industry you're targeting — "anything in marketing" is not a target. Set a daily schedule and stick to it. Spend 20% of your time applying to posted jobs and 80% networking and building relationships. Track every application, every contact, every follow-up.

If Nothing Is Moving After 60 Days

Something in your approach isn't working. Use the Three-Lever Diagnosis: every stalled search has a problem in exactly one of three places, and once you identify which lever is broken, the fix becomes obvious.

Lever one: Targeting. You're applying to the wrong jobs — too senior, too junior, wrong industry, wrong geography, or roles that require skills you don't have. Sign: you apply to many jobs and hear nothing. Fix: narrow your target, apply to fewer things that are a stronger match.

Lever two: Materials. Your resume or LinkedIn isn't converting. Sign: you're applying to jobs that seem like a fit but getting no response, or you're getting first-round calls but nothing after. Fix: get someone blunt to review your resume. Have someone read your LinkedIn profile cold and tell you what impression it leaves.

Lever three: Relationships. You're not talking to enough people. Sign: most of your activity is online, you're spending more time applying than having conversations, your network has gone quiet. Fix: the Job Search Inversion — flip your ratio back to 80% conversations, 20% applications.

Most people try to fix all three at once, which means they fix none of them. Be honest about which lever is actually broken. Then fix that one thing.

When You Land the Job

Negotiate before you accept. Start building your emergency fund back up immediately — six months of expenses minimum. Keep your resume current from day one. Stay in touch with your network; don't disappear now that you don't need anything. Help the next person who goes through this. You know what it's actually like. That knowledge is worth something. And start practicing Always-On Readiness now, while you have the luxury of time. The four components are simple: resume current within 30 days, LinkedIn active, five real external relationships, three months cash minimum. Do them from the first week of your new job, not the week after you lose it.

About the Author

Richard Lowe spent 20 years as Director of Computer Operations at Trader Joe's — a $16 billion company with 474 stores and 38,000 employees. He built hiring teams, ran two complete digital transformations, managed the infrastructure that kept a national retail chain running, and sat across the table from enough job candidates to know exactly what hiring managers are actually thinking.

Before Trader Joe's, he was VP of Consulting at two technology firms, managed SCADA systems for major water utilities, and led the development of one of the first fraud detection systems ever built for the telecom industry. He has been building things and managing people since 1980.

He also knows unemployment from the inside. When he left corporate life in 2013, he had to rebuild his professional identity from scratch at an age when most people assume the hard part is behind them. That experience — combined with two decades of watching people get hired and fired — is what this book is built on.

Since then, Richard has become a ghostwriter with 113+ published books. His clients include Fortune 50 executives who secured $30 million in venture capital, CEOs who landed TEDx stages, and professionals who went from overlooked to recruited after a single book repositioned them. One of his books sold 15,000 copies in three days and has been translated into seven languages. His work has been adopted as a required textbook at Purdue University.

Richard has appeared on 55+ podcasts including The Chris Voss Show, hosts his own podcast "Leaders and Their Stories," and has spoken at Purdue University's entrepreneurship program for four consecutive years. He lives in Florida, builds scale model tanks, and has photographed over 300 Renaissance festivals. He has survived three earthquakes, four hurricanes, and a forest fire.

Books by Richard Lowe

See books by Richard Lowe at

https://masterofworlds.com

Get free publishing insights and industry updates at

https://thewritingking.substack.com

For ghostwriting and book coaching services see

https://thewritingking.com

www.ingramcontent.com/pod-product-compliance
Lightning Source LLC
Chambersburg PA
CBHW032026050726
47590CB00006B/2318